The No B.S Truth

What it Takes to Build a Successful Business

Compiled by

Kim Boudreau Smith & Kate Gardner

For more information, visit:

www.kimbsmith.com / www.themissingpiecemagazine.com

Book and cover design by Jennifer Insignares www.yourdesignsbyjen.com

Edited by: Amanda Ni Odhrain http://www.amandahoranediting.weebly.com

Formatted by: Bojan Kratofil https://www.facebook.com/bojan.kratofil

ISBN: 978-1-5136-1719-0

Gratitude Page

Kate: First of all, let me start by showing my appreciation for the ladies in this book, ladies like myself and Kim who had a vision to create our last anthology book featuring a powerful subject. You ladies saw our vision and took our sides to join us for the journey and for that I am so proud and grateful of each one of you. Thank you.

To Kim, my Kimba, my best friend, my business partner and my coach for when I need a swift kick in the pants. It's been one heck of an amazing ride for us over the past 5 years. We know very few remain standing in this industry and to have come the full journey with you creates an unbreakable bond that no person could ever get between. Thank you for being you and I look forward to the journey ahead.

To my amazing partner Matthew, my children Emily & Jordan, and my granddaughter Rosie, and my grandson David in heaven. You are the reason I breath. Thank you for choosing me to be your mother, grandmother and wife.

I am blessed.

Kim: I want to be clear, I am more than thankful for so much in my life and I do not always express it. I live in gratitude, not just being thankful. I live for faith, not just trust. I do not like to be sorry. I apologize when it is a desire, not a necessity. These are my terms, and no one else dictates this.

I have learned that my friendships far and few around the world are my heart and soul. One was compromised and that will not happen again. Kate Gardner, I am grateful for your humor, love, and friendship that is whacky, crazy and so real! Our conversations are crazy with venting, masterminding, and a lot of peeing in our pants laughing! I cannot wait to see what the future holds for you. You are one smart woman and you are not afraid to do the work! I am grateful we finally partnered in a book. This will be our last anthology together, a platform where we met and now a platform that we place to rest as we springboard into bigger things! Whew, what a ride it has been! Now let's ramp up the ride even more.

As I write I look at these amazing co-authors, some I know and some I am just getting to know. What a great group of women. I am a believer in surrounding yourself with like-minded women from all walks of life and Kate and I have done just that with this group. I am excited and grateful for all of them to be a part of this book. We couldn't have done it without all 16 of them! Ladies, I am grateful and stand in awe.

This project's team is outstanding. The cliché goes "Behind every great man stands a woman," well I believe that behind every great business owner/leader, stands right beside them an amazing team! How else can we manage such a large project? You all rock!

I have had some amazing people come into my life all by the way of social media. There are too many to mention, but I love you all. You know who you are! Each and every one of you has placed footprints on my heart, inspired me, and lifted me up when needed, and also laughed with me and cheered me on. Most importantly, you all are just amazing beings!

Always last but not the least, thank you to my husband Steve. Much gratitude and appreciation. Oh, and yes Steve I guess you really are not last, my two assistants, Grace and Luna. Grace, my amazing Grace, you show kindness and patience and Luna, oh boy, such a tiny barrel of love, fun, and puppy-ness! My gorgeous girls that teach me a lot.

I am whole!

Table of Contents

Kate's Introduction

Isn't it so funny how when I sat down to write this book and tell you the about the truth about my success, that I sat here for a moment and thought to myself "Is the reader really ready for this?" … Are they ready to hear the truth?

Of course, you are! Otherwise you wouldn't have bought the book in the first place, right? Everybody comes into our lives for a reason, and my reason for me coming into your life right now is because of this book. To give you the truth and nothing but the truth, so that you can go on your journey to build your online business clued up with the knowledge that you need to hear. So, in hope that my costly and painful mistakes don't become your own, and above all to inspire you to let you know that all dreams can become reality if you are willing to work your ass off and become a better person each day.

There will be zero bullshit in this book and just like my solo authored business book *The Missing Piece in Online Business: Great Expert Advice That Will Save You from Going Broke*, it will contain the best business advice that you could possible need on your journey to success. It's time to go that deeper level and tell you what it's like to be a CEO of an online company. The sacrifices that you have to make, the blood sweat and tears that you must place into something to make it a success, and to prepare you for what is about to come. This is something a lot of people DON'T DO! It takes courage and big lady balls to be completely honest with people. To take a stand and tell them "how it is" in this industry. So, welcome to the truth of understanding why you need to read this book before you begin to even think about upleveling and building that 6-figure empire.

Firstly, there are a few home truths that you need to hear and not just from my side, but from other people as well. I didn't want you to receive a one-sided view on this I wanted you to see how success, passion and purpose effects those all around you too. That is why myself and Kim invited other women business owners to share their experiences to help fetch you the truth! Which you will find all the above and more right here in *The B.S Truth: What it Really Takes to Succeed in Business!*

With much love & appreciation

Kate Gardner

17 x International Best-Selling author & Editor of The Missing Piece Magazine

www.themissingpiecemagazine.com

Kim's Introduction

I decided in the beginning of 2016 it was time for one more anthology to make it three under my belt, and then I was finished. Halfway through I decided to pull the plug, but I received such disappointment from the women that were all ready to participate. I knew I couldn't do that to them - breaking my commitment wasn't an option. This is when Kate and I decided to stop talking our talk about partnering up on projects and really walk this talk. So together we decided to change things from our past anthologies, scale down, customize even more and then retire from these projects. So we are going out with a bang in 2016 and taking along some amazing women with us on this ride.

This book is about all the B.S. in business, actually in life, that people are just afraid to talk about. As a result, we have people still feeling alone, lost, quitting, losing hope, burnt-out and so much more. On the other side of all of this is the BULLSHIT that is out there via social media. The fakeness, the 'wannabes,' copy-cats and laziness. People desperate and wanting a business overnight that is cheap, liars, broke (in so many ways) and not keeping to their commitment which in turn has a devastating rippling effect on all of us! Did you ever think of that?

Please do not misunderstand me here, this is not a book on bitching, bashing and such, this is a book on how we keep going even though we have been hit with all the bullshit out there. How do we rise above, learn from all of this and show up 100% strong and committed? The NO B.S. in Business will inspire you to keep on keeping on and show up without all the B.S. baggage of your own and everyone else's. How to truly navigate a business. It takes Boldness, bravery and courage, personal development, MONEY, yes money, passion and never ending passion, insight, and support from others, inner wisdom and the ability to surrender to the universe. There is a plan for all of us out there, but we must clean up the bullshit in our lives EVERY SINGLE DAY!

Sound exhausting? If you answered yes, then maybe you better find another avenue to drive down because owning a business is not for the faint hearted! Listen, this book isn't to scare you away, it is to open your eyes, your heart, and to develop a thick skin to get out there. All this stuff you see on social media isn't what it appears to be! Create your own world. Don't copy what someone else is doing. There is no guarantee that it will work for you. It is like wearing shoes, one size and style doesn't fit everyone!

Please enjoy removing the B.S. from your life with this book. You are meant to have your dreams on your terms without all the cheap people, the fakes, the liars and the wannabes!

Remember, do not quit, and do not give up. Take a different route to your destination. Sometimes we need to do that. The picture of our dream does not always show up how we want it. Be open and surrender to the bigger picture, but remember to do the work!

Kim Boudreau Smith

Kim Boudreau Smith is a multi-talented CEO and business leader with a legacy of empowering thousands of women. From a corporate background in sales and marketing and over 20 years of experience in the fitness industry, Kim has gone on to become an #1 international best-selling author with the book being one of the best-selling on Amazon for 2015! Kim also has become a multiple international best-selling author, business consultant and speaker.

Kim combines her expertise with a passion to motivate and inspire other women to become "Top producers in their lives." As CEO of Kim Boudreau Smith Inc.& Bold Radio Station her international speaking and coaching work has enabled thousands of women to benefit from her inspirational and empowering work.

Website: www.kimbsmith.com

Chapter 1

Oh, My B.S. is Everywhere!

By Kim Boudreau Smith

I have always said to Kate, we will partner on a book someday and here we are. This book, the title, and the amazing contents are so spot on and Kate and I knew within a phone conversation that we had to lead a No B.S. book for all of the business owners, or shall I say people, that there is a lot of bullshit, ups, and downs in owning a business.

I am here to say all of this B.S. is looking at me and facing my truths, responsibilities, boundaries and not lowering myself to accommodate someone else. When I do just that it hits me-all the B.S.

Being an online business owner for 7 years now has really opened me up to a lot of people with a lot of B.S. It took me some time to realize that many of these people that are claiming to be viable business owners cannot afford to pay a $25.00 invoice. What is wrong with this picture? Or coaches claiming you will fail and not get your business to the next level of clients if you do not buy their five-figure program. Now we all need help and yes we need a business coach of sorts, but will you really die or fail if you do not invest five figures in your business? I do not think so and yes there may be a time when you will need to do that, but be clear on your direction, not desperate. I see people running and hiding behind social media and portraying something that they are not.

So much lack of responsibility going on, blaming and of course victimhood. A lot of desperation which leads to desperate people and decisions. When things blow up we blame others....As Aerosmith sings: *Same Ole Song and Dance!*

I started getting these hits about 5 years ago, working with women, to lead, support, and collaborate with them. So much excites me to the nth degree and back; however, we, as a gender, are lacking a lot. We didn't have other female mentors when we were younger. We want to lead, but continue to buy into the lack of acceptance from spouses, friends, kids and everyone else so we cry, act like a victim and quit. (Why even start to begin with?) After all of that, then we take down another woman because we lack confidence and are jealous so in turn the female gender really has not arrived if one woman still continues to do this. Trust me, it has been done to me time and time again.

Do you know that I bring women together to partner, support and collaborate because "Alone we are smart; together we are brilliant!" ~ Steven Anderson. Yes, I have been called every name in the book, blamed for others' mishaps because they cannot pay an invoice, show up strong or even show up at all. Not only that but then all the personal bullshit comes along. I must ask, are they the only ones with a life? Dealing with stress? Sick dog or kids and so on? I do not even know how to respond to that anymore. If you claim to be a leader, first stop talking about it and show up as one without all the personal baggage. Lean into the business world!

As I am writing this chapter, I am revisiting *The Four Agreements* by Don Miguel Ruiz. He talks about our word; be impeccable with your word. I couldn't agree more with this, but how do we do this when we are wearing the wardrobe of victim-hood? Listen! If you commit to something, stick to it. I find women who believe it is easier to quit, not take responsibility and blame. I see this quite a lot. If owning and building a successful business was easy, there would be more people doing it, wouldn't you say? So get up off your ass and stop with all the B.S. and begin with yourself! Begin with YOUR word to YOU impeccably! Let's talk about this...

We all have a voice in our heads and I call her the Bitch or Hag in the Attic! You know she has been running the show for our whole lives? She doesn't want you to take risks or be responsible. She has bought into the Book of Laws for Life. She wants us to be a robot, numb, unhappy and conformed to what society says to be. What she really wants is to be given boundaries, guided and she needs to be reassured that YOU are the one in charge. This is what you can do to grow into leadership!

Now where to begin? Well get real and become impeccable with yourself and your word to YOU first and foremost. This means you place your head down on your pillow every night knowing you have done your best without excuses and with mistakes, or better known as, lessons. NO PERFECTION here! Our word manifests our reality, so stop and do a reality check. What's up? Feel sick and tired all the time? Or are you saying you are not lucky at all and cannot catch a break? (Okay that is a load of bullshit right there.) Are you running around comparing, striving for acceptance or implementing what everyone else is doing? Whatever happened to, "Do what works for you on your terms?" It is your power of the word, the spoken word, to yourself first and foremost and nothing else. I love when women say they can show up, support other women and they cannot even support themselves. Wow, a volcano waiting to explode there! It cannot be possible to support others in this situation when in fact you are not supporting yourself. We want to be accepted however we do not accept ourselves. We want to lead but we cannot lead ourselves.

We wish for everything outside of us to be happy and we are a hot mess on the inside and take zero responsibility and or actions on this. Ask yourself these questions:

When was the last time you looked in the mirror and said I love You from head to toe inside-out?

What practices do you do in the morning to set your hag in the attic (mindset), your word, and your overall health?

Who, what, when and where do you partner with to enhance your leadership skills, your business and yourself so in turn you can support others? Pay it forward! Serve!

Do you like to tell others how to run themselves when in fact you don't even do this advice you are dishing out?

Really, truly, how do you feel deep down inside of yourself, right now in this moment, the truth, the whole truth and nothing but the truth?

Are you squirming yet reading these questions? Did you skim over them? Not sitting so well with you? Go back and spend some time with each question...

Every day we look into mirrors, superficial mirrors for make-up, hair and driving to name a few, however, we do not spend the REAL NITTY GRITTY time there as much as we need to. This is a daily practice and some days will be easier than others. Just begin, embrace everything about yourself. No good or bad here it is all miraculous, however, we bow down to misery and smallness. Then the novel of the woe is me follows....Now that is B.S.!

The morning is a gift, and every day is a gift of opportunities. How do you set that pace? Wake up grumpy because you hate this or that. Talk negative to yourself all the way to the coffee cup? Waste time or sleep in until the last very second? Do you know that a new day is a new opportunity? Every single day we get an opportunity to go at it again. Here is where you can care for yourself physically, mentally and emotionally by getting a workout in; meditating, and eating a healthy breakfast. What goes into our bodies, heart, mind and soul comes out. ALWAYS! Some way or another through your language and health. A great leader takes the morning and seizes it with joy so they can lead and empower others. Quit showing up empty and loaded with a bunch of B.S. in hand! No one wants it.

When was the last time you invested in yourself? I don't just mean money investment, truly invest in yourself? I do this every day, yes every day! I do not want to hear you don't have the time, which is complete bullshit! When was the last time you joined a group of women to lead, support, and network? How about mentoring? I just mentioned a few things here that didn't need monetary investment, so cut the B.S. and jump in or get out.

I love this. Everyone has advice and knows it all, but is dying on the inside by not practicing what they are preaching. Need I say more? Try mastering everything, it will lead to being a jackass of all trades and keep YOU further away from YOU!

Reading this are you jittery? Saying things to yourself like, well she doesn't have to worry about that, she has a successful business and blah, blah, blah. STOP, that is just plain bullshit and you show up with that.

Listen, I have 3 successful business, but I have taken a lot of hits, financially, emotionally and mentally. I don't take it anymore. I have set up strong boundaries and I play on my terms. Everything from my impeccable word, customer service, payments, investments, and I am raw and real. I have been blamed for destroying business deals in just three days. That is B.S., I do not have the power to do that, so there wasn't anything there to begin with. I have been blamed I do not pay my bills when in fact I do and that person who said that owes me a lot of money. You see, I have learned not to take anything personally. This is the second agreement in *The Four Agreements*. This is a tough hone for me, and it takes work and a lot of practice. Everything that I am being accused of and called, I know it is that person's issue not mine. You cannot possibly know what I can or cannot do. You can only know what you are capable of doing and no one else. But we blame and bring all the bull shit into the outside world. Trust me, you will always struggle for money, clients, and a successful and happy life if you continue to do this. Face the truth, stop the façade and quit faking it until you make it. A terrible cliché to live by.

Show up strong and courageous. Stop worrying what others are thinking, because you will never know. Build your personal empire based upon your dream and vision, not anyone else's Do what works for you and your clients. Life is not a one stop shop nor is the business. So stop watching, comparing and trying to do what others do. It isn't you! Until you live, breathe and walk this way you will always be in the bullshit!

Kate Gardner

Kate Gardner is a 17 x International Best-Selling Author and Editor of The Missing Piece Magazine and Publisher of the International Best-Selling Book Series; The Missing Piece.

As a coach Kate helps raise her client's self-esteem and self-confidence through providing tools and platforms to help present themselves professionally to their audience to enable them to gain the attention and sales they deserve. Over the last 3 years Kate has helped nearly 200 authors becoming best-selling authors by teaching them how to publish books and make their book a best seller. Kate has had the honor of working with TV personalities and award winning film directors.

Website: www.themissingpiecemagazine.com

Publishing Consulting: www.ayearofchange.com

Chapter 2

Facing the Truth

By Kate Gardner

The idea for this book came to me in a conversation with Kim one day. I slept on it overnight and as soon as the sun rose the next day and it was time to wake up I bounced out of bed, ran into my office and wrote down the parts I would need to include.

Something hit me in the moment while I was writing the notes down, and that was I must face the truth of my dreams, and when they tell me something I must carry it out. It's a map of visions that I should be creating in my reality. I decided there and then I was going to face more responsibility and face the truth of my dreams as well.

This was me facing a little more responsibility in my life than I had done before and that is what all this journey is about. How much more truth are you going to face daily? Are you going to face the truth completely? Or still run away and hide from it?

Every day I see people running and hiding from the one person they can't stand to be 100% honest with and that is THEM SELVES! Please don't be one of these people that runs and hides at every problem and if you choose to be that person, please remember that whatever you place out to the world will come back and bite you on the ass big time!

If you choose to be a leader, then take the responsibility for that choice! Don't play the blame game and be a victim. Don't blame other people for your issues. We all create the reality we have by the choices we have made along the way and if your reality sucks balls big time right now, well guess what? You made it like that and it's now up to you to place your big girl/boy pants on and make bigger and better choices, so that 3 months down the line you are not the one left in the crap again.

If you think it's harsh that I am speaking to you like this now, then just think what I would be like as your coach? I spare no room for excuses or the victim mind-set because I used to be a victim myself. My mind was conditioned all the way through childhood to be just like society intended. Broke, ill and stuck on a hamster wheel to please everybody else around me but myself and live a miserable life.

Life changes dramatically when you stand up and say "Fuck this." I choose not to rot away in front of a TV every night after slogging my guts out in a dead end 9-5 job, nor do I choose to live in debt to society while they ram TV commercials down my throat to slowly brain wash my mind so that I purchase meaningless crappy material things, kill my relationship with my partner and kids and I die only leaving an arm chair full of moth balls and an indentation where my arse crack use to be!

NO! I choose to ditch all that, work on myself every single day to become a better person, serve humanity and build a legacy so that for generations to come. I inspire my family to know that just by taking responsibility for your life and facing the truth, you can do anything you want! You can make your dreams become REAL!

But first you must face the truth.........Are you ready to do that?

Run yourself through the questions below and pay attention to how you FEEL when you answer them. If your first reaction is to reject them while answering them, then, my friend I'm afraid there is more work to be done on your part of facing the truth.

1) When you ask for advice from others do you instantly reject the feedback?

2) Do you place a negative statement from your past into most conversations?

3) Are you not earning any money in your business right now?

4) Are you feeling frustrated over money?

5) Can you say you are truly happy in your business?

6) Do you launch things into the world and they don't sell?

7) Do you feel so overwhelmed with work?

8) Are your relationships suffering?

9) Is your health suffering?

10) Do you feel like people should be buying from you and they are not?

Some of the answers to these questions may be quite hard to bear and you may not want to answer them truthfully because you wish to detach yourself away from the emotional raw pain of the truth. Facing the truth is not easy and believe I know because I have had to encounter one slap in the face after another to get to where I am today.

I didn't wake up one morning to become a CEO of a successful brand with a wonderful team around me. I had to work hard at facing the truth every single day by dealing with my problems and not running away from the biggest 10 issues I listed above, which I see struggling business owners going through day in day out. I am afraid there is no magic wand for you to wave to make it all bright and amazing for you. You must face the reality of these things one step at a time to help grow that thick skin so that you can deal with it all and do what needs to be done to make it right. Even when it's admitting you are in the wrong!

So, let's go through the list of 10 things again, only this time list where you need to face the truth in every situation.

1) When you ask for advice from others do you instant reject the feedback?

I want you to go back through your social media posts of you asking an opinion of your following. It could be that you asked them what they thought of your brand-new program cover, sales page, website, or book cover. Then I want you to re-read the comments that you replied to. Are you considering what these people are saying to you? Or are you rejecting any statement they are giving?

You must remember that when you are in business the person you sell to needs to be heard in the first place and if you are not willing to face the truth of their feedback then it's game over for you right from the start. By going back over your own comments and replies to the feedback it's going to hit home how big your ego is and if you have not faced the truth about what your customers are telling you.

There is no bigger turn off on this planet than a business owner who thinks what they are doing is brilliant when really, nobody knows what they are taking about. If you have that kind of perception you are living in a dream world and need to seriously cart yourself into an ego bashing class for beginners and sign up for a whole 10-year course!

The planet you live on is constantly evolving and so is the social society we live in. We communicate differently now than we did 5 years ago. Social media has taken over business, social lives, relationships, the way we interact and the way we buy things. It's the main dominator for consumers across the globe. So, if you are not going to sit there and face the truth of what people say to you and still use 'what you think works' then you will be staying stagnant for a heck of a lot of time to come.

Keep up with the pace of social media marketing by asking what your people think and deliver what they want…. It's that simple! Serving humanity is about firstly facing the truth that our journey is not about us, and then it's about asking what these people want and then delivering the solutions.

2) Do you place a negative statement from your past into most conversations?

How to spot a victim mind-set in 2.5 seconds? Every conversation will have a drag back statement. What do I mean by a dragged back statement? A drag back statement is what I just made up on the spot for them. Annoying statements like:

"It could be worse you could have _____." (Fill in with whatever B.S. story you like.)

"Yeah but least you haven't ever _____." (Again fill in with any B.S. story you like.)

Drag back statements are something that people fetch into their current reality because they haven't yet let go and moved on. They don't want to let go of the bad things that have happened to them in the past and nor do they want to face the home truths of why their life isn't the way they want it right now. So instead they moan, bitch, complain and drag something back from their past in hope for you to feel sorry for them and feed off your guilt.

My advice on this one is if you are a person who wants to be successful then you need to face the truth on this one and ditch these kind of people, or forgive your own past issues and never drag them past situations back into your future within normal everyday conversations.

You are no longer a victim to circumstance, you are a leader and building a legacy, so forgive them, forgive yourself, and let the shit go!

3) Are you not earning any money in your business right now?

Are you frustrated because you have more money going out then you have coming in? Or maybe you are not earning anything at all? Not a bean! Not a sausage!

I will tell you a complete straight up honest reply to this! **STOP focusing on money!**

All that energy and focus you are wasting on worrying about money is consuming your life, when that energy needs to be focused on building a powerful brand with respectful foundations. The only way you are going to get them respectful foundations is if you LOOK at what people are telling you. All the clues are in the conversation you have with your following. If you are seeing comments like;

"I am so overwhelmed right now."

"I need to shed a few pounds."

"I need to be kept accountable for things."

"I wish I had a great website."

"I wish I knew all this techy stuff."

"I would love to be organised right now."

"I want to feel more positive."

This is your cue to SERVE HUMANITY It is up to YOU to find the answers and within finding the solutions for these people you will be REWARDED. So, let's face the truth here and realise that no matter what it takes you learn those solutions and SERVE like you are suppose too. Then you will see a massive shift in everything you do.

People all around you are telling you their problems and you as their teacher, mentor, or coach must learn the skills and do exactly what you were born to do: TEACH! So, go take whatever class is necessary to discover these solutions and use that energy that you have been focusing on 'how much you haven't had for so long' and turn it into the skills you need to serve these people so you can be rewarded for your time.

4) Are you feeling frustrated over money?

Take the energy away from what you do not have and focus how you can make it happen. Money is the biggest dominator of humanity and without we are pretty much screwed. However, if you choose to focus on 'lack of' rather than how much you are going to earn this year and how you are going to do it? Then, like I said in the previous statement you are wasting energy in the wrong part of your life.

Face the truth, responsibility and see that it is down to you to make the money flow in and not anybody else.

5) Can you say you are truly happy in your business?

Does your business make you cry happy tears? Fill a hole so deep with satisfaction of serving that every time you see lives touched by your creative work your heart swells?

No? Then my darling we have some home truths to face here and #1 priority is if you are miserable or confused and have no idea what you should be doing, or you are just down right miserable then you still have a mass load of conditioning to unravel in that mind-set of yours. You need to find out who you truly are deep down inside, so that you can gain massive clarity and begin to understand your true purpose.

You must see yourself doing what you do for the next 60 years or more and feel like the only time you will retire is when you are dead because you love doing what you do so much. The pits of your tummy will burn and ignite like a coal fire. The coals will burn so hot that you will have steam coming off you.

True happiness in your work is like a magnet to clients and when they truly see that you love what you do because it shines out of you like a lighthouse lamp, then you will know you are right where you are supposed to be.

6) Do you launch things into the world and they don't sell?

This comes under you not listening and realising that you should be selling to your following what they want and not want you think they want. To become a great sales person (because that is what every business owner is) you must listen to your customer.

Ask them how they would like to see a product launched? What do they find attractive on a sales page? Which marketing from which brand speaks the most to them? And why? All this is placing you more responsible for your business, life and your customer's needs. So, when in doubt ask the audience!

7) Do you feel so overwhelmed with work?

Are you feeling like screaming "OH MY GOD I will never get all this done?" This is you taking on far too much, being dis-organised and going down the self-sabotage route of not having very much respect for yourself.

If you are overwhelmed or otherwise known as 'busy' then you need to STOP! Take a deep breath and have more respect for your mental wellbeing. If you are in this state of mind right now then you think how it's effecting everybody around you and consider that anything you write, pitch, or coach and teach will be an extension of how you are feeling inside. You will get irritable with people, have less time for people, mistakes will be made, and it all could have been easily controlled if you had just stopped and planned exactly what 5 goals you were going to carry out that day. Balance your day with 5 things you need to get done and once they are out of the way place the other things in your life forward. It you decide to sit there all day on your laptop and ignore the people close to you then don't freak out one day when they leave you because you lost all appreciation for them and immersed yourself too far deep that you forgot about those around you!

8) Are your relationships suffering?

Is your favourite phrase to your husband/wife and kids "Yeah I will be there in a minute" and five hours later you are still at your computer? This carries on from the last question I asked and makes you identify that keeping yourself 'busy' instead of scheduled can ruin your relationships.

We must face the truth more when it comes to relationships suffering and understand that it's not us taking responsibility for our schedules, and by not doing so all those around us are suffering. My whole life is scheduled from the minute I wake up to the moment I go to bed, but then it needs to be because if I don't face the truth and keep myself in check then my whole company would be in the drain and my family life would be in the toilet.

Yes, I may have 3 schedules, a training schedule, media schedule and work schedule, but this just shows how committed I am to not waste time and sit there with my thumb up my arse making excuses to why my life isn't the way I want it. Instead I plan 12 months ahead and schedule everything so it gets done!

9) Is your health suffering?

Self-care is something that around 85% of the population on the planet put last in their lives. We feel we must place everything and everyone before ourselves and drain ourselves from exhaustion to the point we get sick. Then we are of no use to anyone and then feel even guiltier for having to take time out to rest and heal.

High self-respect is essential when you have a passion and purpose to serve humanity. If the levels of self-respect are so low for yourself then you will only keep attracting the same thing too you. You don't want to attract clients that will walk all over you, pay you when they want to and give you a whole bunch of grief towards it.

You only have one body and you cannot trade it in for a new one. This is it! The body you have been given needs to see you through your entire life and how you respect yourself will indeed result in what you attract, how you feel and your health.

Do what makes you feel good, have high self-respect for yourself, and never feel guilty for placing yourself first.

10) Do you feel like people should be buying from you and they are not?

Guilty as charged right here! I started out in online business 5 years ago wondering why the heck people where not buying from me? Oblivious to the fact online business is a whole new ball game from offline business, and that it is something that keeps evolving day in day out and if you don't keep up you will get left behind.

Your free time should be used up wisely by learning new skills in online marketing, copy writing and a whole host of other skills. Learning does not need to be expensive you just need to be willing and prepared to do what others don't.

Take an hour or two out a week to learn new skills, hire people who have what you truly desire and ask them to teach you how.

Nothing changes until you apply change to your life and if I was still the person I was 5 years ago, then my life wouldn't be where it is today. You only have one life, make it count.

Alison Donaghey

Thought strategist. What an ideal way to describe Alison Donaghey; a successful business owner, author and speaker. Alison challenges people to think about what they think about and to *think opposite* at least once a day. She can share countless examples of how encouraging others to question their status quo often leads to improvements not only in *their* world but *the* world. Her international #1 best-selling book Change Your Business, Change the World: The Domino Effect of Your Thinking is changing lives in ways Alison never even thought of.

Website: www.Dominothinking.com

Chapter 3

Think Opposite to Survive the Good, The Bad and The Ugly of Business.

By Alison Donaghey

I don't think I knew I wanted to own my own business until I was a couple of years into owning it!

This is what I did know:

- I didn't want my hour having a price tag attached to it.

- I wanted to have the ability to make more than my wage in an hour if I worked harder.

- I didn't want someone deciding what I was worth.

- I wanted freedom (or at least a perception of freedom!).

- I wanted flexibility.

- Decision making was important to me.

In short, autonomy had a huge value for me.

I came from a family that played by the rules. My dad worked for the city. My mom worked for a financial institution. They divorced when I was in grade 6, and my mom remarried. When that happened, we moved across Canada to the west coast. Unfortunately, we moved just before the recession, and neither my mom nor my stepdad were established. My stepdad took jobs when he could find them and my mom worked on a casual basis doing office work when she could find it. Jobs were scarce and I remember feeling suffocated by their financial restrictions. I learned that money was attached to freedom.

At age 20 I gave birth to my son. I had never held a baby until he was born. It was a steep learning curve, to say the least!

By the time he was a year old I had separated from his father. It was a really good move for me, as his father contributed very little. I went from one job to another but never enough to get completely off welfare. I didn't have a lot of control over my choices. I really didn't like that (yep that autonomy thing!).

In 1992, I decided that if I was going to get out of this dead-end routine, I should go back to school. Probably not the route I would recommend today but was certainly the best option at the time. I enrolled full-time study in criminology and worked three part-time jobs to make ends meet. Even then, I was still dependant on welfare for help with daycare.

In 1994, I met a guy (how many stories have been told with some variation of that sentence?). He painted houses and told me that if I learned how to paint, I could make more money and see my son more often. Hell yeah! Where do I sign up?

To cut a long story short, this guy relapsed into drug addiction. He died in 1999 and left me over $10,000 in debt. I was still dependant on welfare to some extent, but I made a choice to *think opposite.* I made a conscious decision to go against the status quo, which was to get a job without autonomy, like almost everyone else.

Instead, I decided to start a painting company. I called it Sonshine Girls Painting; *Son*shine because I have a son and *Girls* because when, as a female, I was treated so poorly by staff and customers when I painted for Bob. I figured if *Girls* was in the title all those people who thought women couldn't do things just wouldn't call me.

I knew nothing about business, estimating, and really nothing about painting except how to put it on the walls; minor details right? I had no plan, no marketing, and no idea how complex it was *supposed* to be.

I have to say, this was the most amazing thing about being young. I operated on the idea that I knew everything and could do anything. Aging takes that away from us a bit. It replaces over-confidence with knowledge. The more we know, the more there is to be afraid of, despite evidence of our ability to accomplish. It's a conundrum.

So what is my version of the good, the bad and the ugly (and not necessarily in that order) of owning a business?

THE BAD

I had to work really long hours in order to be successful and get off welfare. This meant that I didn't often get to sit around the house and play with my son or volunteer at his school. It meant I didn't have time to cultivate friendships, but I suspect that disappeared long before I started my business.

I didn't have a steady reliable income. At the end of every paint job I was unemployed. This was nerve wracking.

I had to hire staff. Anyone who has staff knows it really is a love/hate relationship. Finding that balance between business and personal is hard.

THE UGLY

I discovered that I was not welcome in this male dominated trade. I quickly learned when I would ask questions of other painters they would often lie to me. As a result, I had almost no one I could learn from.

I had people judging my choice to start my own business. People close to me would say "When are you going to get a real job?"

The self-doubt was at times crippling.

THE GOOD

Well this list could go on forever! But for the sake of continuity my top three picks are as follows:

I had autonomy.

The amount of effort I put in directly reflected the amount of money I made.

I created a really good life.

THE STORY

My first year I had no external way to measure my success. I didn't know what other companies were making, because I had no one to ask. There was no Internet to research these things and, to be perfectly honest, I was just too busy to have found the time even if the internet did exist. All I knew was that my customers said they were happy. I was able to pay my bills and failing wasn't an option.

Let's be real, making enough money to get off welfare was not a high bar to set. At the time it seemed very daunting, but the reality was I only had to get a couple of jobs. Eventually those couple of jobs led to more, and I got to hire my first employee.

My first attempts at hiring staff were disasters. I thought I should be grateful for whoever wanted to work with me. Of course with a company name like Sonshine Girls Painting, there were not too many men willing to be a Sonshine Girl, and there were not too many female painters at that time.

I realized that in order to find staff I had to start to *think opposite* of how I had been thinking. I didn't have to be grateful for someone wanting to work for me. I needed to find someone who was grateful to have a good job where we could have fun too! I did find a woman who was very interested in painting but had no experience. It was then that I learned that experience is overrated. After all, I had none at one point and now I owned a company. Willingness. *That* is something I wanted in a painter. *That* cannot be taught. So I taught her to paint, and she showed up willing, and we worked really well together. Well enough that I could return to finish my final year of university.

It had always bothered me that I hadn't finished my degree. I had my diploma in criminology and three years towards my degree, but with Bob's drug addiction, returning to finish had not been an option. Now, it was an option. Honestly I still wasn't thinking of myself like a business owner and part of me still thought I could get a 'real' job if I finished my degree.

I met with Student Services at university to see what finishing would look like. They told me I couldn't run a company and finish all my courses in a year. I talked to my friends and they told me I was crazy. Again, I decided to *think opposite* and I took my full course load. I finished my degree with a 3.33 GPA, not the coveted 4.0, but not bad for a single mom running a business.

At that point I was feeling pretty comfortable with my company and thought I would like to travel. I knew I wasn't making enough money to just travel, so I thought I could teach English while I was doing it. I took a full time course to get my CELTA (ESL training) and landed a job in Italy. Oh man! Be careful what you wish for. I had been successful missing hours in my work day for school, but leaving the country was quite another thing.

I sold everything and I left my employee in charge. Every day we would connect (the phone bills were astronomical) and I would talk her through estimates, banking and problems. Mostly, it worked. I got extremely sick in Italy so my son and I had to move back to Canada. He was pretty happy about that because he missed his friends. My employee wasn't as crazy about it. Our relationship fell apart and we parted ways.

Each year business got better. Within 5 years of conception of the business I had my first 100K year and my house was paid off. Life was good. I was travelling. I was able to take time off to do things with my son. In his grade 12 year I went to every single home and away game in his basketball season. I didn't have to miss anything. I still worked stupid long hours, but I got to choose when that happened and what that looked like.

I thought I was a rock star at this business thing. Alas, in 2009 the economy tanked. It was a super humbling experience for me. I wasn't such a rock star after all; I had been riding the wave of the good economy. Businesses were shutting down all over the place, but I was fortunate that I had created a really solid foundation for my business. It was this foundation that saved my company, most which was built on my ability to *think opposite.*

2009 was probably the first year I had to really think about business from the financial nuts and bolts perspective. Up until this point I had just been cashing checks, paying bills, and of course the woo-hooing when I had money to pay myself. The jobs kept rolling in. Then they didn't. I still had work because I had a great reputation, but I went from 18 staff to 5 and then to 3. I started to really weigh out my business choices. I began making strategic decisions rather than just winging it.

I looked at my branding and realized I needed a more professional look, so I rebranded. I started tracking my leads and made advertising decisions accordingly. I weighed out the pros and cons of my decisions and always considered alternative perspectives.

By 2012, my company had stabilized again. It was trimmer and more efficient. At this point, the opportunity came to buy a property at a really good price to build a house. Not only did I build the house, I designed it too!

This concept of *think opposite*, to always consider the other side of the coin, not only built my business to be one of the best known in my city, but it saved me during the recession. These are some of the things that it worked:

- I really considered if I needed deposits from my clients. I decided I didn't. It was recommended, but I *thought opposite* and came to the conclusion that deposits make customers nervous and if a client wanted to back out, they could. No harm done. I don't want a client who doesn't want us – for whatever reason. My clients *loved* the trust.

- Industry standard is to let the clients pick their own colours. I realized that more often than not, the client spent money on us without getting a colour they loved, which presented another opportunity to *think opposite*. I started to help clients with their colour selection. Low and behold, they all ended up with colours *I* would choose, not colours *they* would necessarily choose. It was at that point I put all the responsibility with the client by creating a course teaching them how to look at colour (yourperfectcolors.com). I pulled back the curtain and showed them how to avoid the mistakes. My clients *loved* it.

- I gave super detailed estimates outlining exactly what I was bidding on and what they were paying for. This was a *think opposite* occasion. There seemed to be a practice in the industry to tell the client as little as possible. I had a woman call me telling me she wanted me to paint her bathroom for $50. I asked her why only $50? Her reply was that she had a painter come in to paint her entire house and she couldn't decide on the best colour for the bathroom. After painting the bathroom, she didn't like it and asked him to remove it. Having no idea how the cost of the whole job broke down into rooms, the painter said he would take $50 off the bill. I never wanted to be that company, so I changed the way I did estimates. Yes, it took longer and it wasn't the industry norm, but my clients *loved* it.

- I found that my clients had really limited knowledge of paints and painting. I decided to make education a big part of my estimating practice. I know some people like to keep an air of mystery surrounding their trade. I *thought opposite*. For a magician, mystery makes sense. In painting? Not so much. Potential clients may select a different company, but at least they will have learned something along the way, and knowledge is power. They *loved* it.

- I started doing 'love tokens' with my staff. Each Friday between paydays, employees were give 15 virtual tokens to distribute amongst their co-workers, based on how they valued them. The winner of the most tokens got $50 cash. I was amazed by how it changed the dynamic of my team. It taught me who was working and what team members valued in another staff. I surrendered some of the decision making to them and it allowed them to *think opposite* too. By the way - they *loved* it.

These are some of the ways I employed the practice of *think opposite*. This practice was so successful for my company, that I have started helping other people to *think opposite* too. I created a company called Domino Thinking, where I speak and teach about the concept of *think opposite*. I am a thought strategist and just published my first best selling book called *Change Your Business, Change the World: The Domino Effect of Your Thinking*.

I know that when we begin to think differently, doors open and solutions show up. This allows us to be cutting edge in all aspects of our lives. We will think about social policy, politics, fights with those we love, how we talk to our children, and how we talk to *ourselves* differently.

Try this. Think about something you are aware of but not emotionally charged about. If they are emotionally charged for you, pick one that is not. Others, you can tackle when you have a bit of practice! Pick one of your own or one of the following:

- People who tailgate when they drive are jerks.

- Women should be married before they have sex.

- Pro-life is the best choice.

- Death penalty should be reinstated.

- Apple Computers are better than PC

- Rain is horrible.

Pick something, and on one side of a piece of paper write down everything you can think of to support your position. When you have exhausted your list (5 mins) flip the paper over and write down the opposite idea.

- People who tailgate are not jerks.

- Women should have sex when they want.

- Pro-choice is the best choice.

- Death penalty should be abolished.

- PC is better than Apple.

- Rain is splendid.

Now write down anything you can think about to support *that* position.

Once you have a reasonable list, see if there is any validity in the opposition. How do you feel about that? Is there a better way? Look at your original list. Does it still have as much validity as it did when you first wrote it? Ask people you know about this topic. Do they have different comments? Start a conversation where no one is right and no one is wrong.

By doing this you are exercising your brain. By exercising your brain, you are expanding your ability to think about things more fully. Eventually you will be able to *think opposite* with emotionally charged topics too. Imagine how you will argue with your spouse, children, coworkers, business partner or anyone else you may encounter, differently if you can pause and think about things from their perspective. You may still be right but you may soften a bit which will lessen the blow of the argument.

I built my first business based on *think opposite*. I considered both sides of each coin and created policies reflecting the outcome. I stopped being married to *my* way as *the* only way, which opened up a whole new way of living for me and an opportunity to do things better. I am building my second business by helping people to apply *think opposite* to their life and their business, so they too, can consider both sides of the same coin before acting on a thought.

The good, the bad and the ugly in business is unavoidable. The way you approach it directly contributes to your level of success. *Think opposite* can maximize the good in business and minimize the bad and ugly.

Allison Tuffs

Allison Tuffs is on a mission to empower women to redefine their life. Following the loss of her daughter Allison experienced 5 years of pain, exhaustion and life dissatisfaction. In 2014, after carotid artery surgery, she decided to take control of her body and life.

Self-empowerment and self-trust were key to healing her body and growing her confidence and self-esteem. Today, Allison has dedicated her life to educating women so they too can make daily choices that will energize and fulfill them.

Allison is an open and inspiring speaker, and energizing leader that brings heart to every conversation.

Website: http://www.allisontuffs.com

https://www.facebook.com/UpYourEnergy/

https://ca.linkedin.com/in/allison-tuffs-35b735a

Chapter 4

3 Success Strategies for Business and Lifestyle Balance

By Allison Tuffs

On May 28, 2009 my daughter passed away. I didn't know how to process the unbearable pain of loss so I swept my feelings under the carpet, put her things in a closet, and dove head first into my career. It soared and I accepted promotion after promotion. Life was great, or so it seemed on the outside.

Life wasn't great! My body was slowly failing; I was disconnected from my family, my body and my happiness.

Shortly after Katerina's death health shifts started to occur. First it was exhaustion, pain, hot flashes, diarrhea and failing memory. Then in January of 2014, on her birthday, I was diagnosed with a brain and carotid artery aneurysm. Later that night, I looked to the sky, held my hands up and said aloud to her, "I'm listening." The time had come. I could no longer run, I turned and faced my greatest fears.

Since that moment, I've been tearing down walls and building a new life. I've drawn on every ounce of knowledge acquired during my Masters and Bachelor of Science in Nutrition and MBA, to rebuild my body and spirit and to launch a new career.

I've been in business now for 2 years, during which I've faced obstacles and climbed many mountains. The biggest impact on my business has been identifying and working on three key areas.

1. Get rid of your luggage and deal with your stuff.

2. Keep on top of your energy as that is what fuels you to move forward in your business and in life.

3. Treat your business like a business and others will too.

In essence, it all came down to the decisions I made which catapulted or plummeted my business.

Let's journey back to 2014.

My life was rapidly transforming. I was dissatisfied at work, my health had tanked and I was desperately seeking freedom.

I dreamt of the freedom to live fully, to raise my children, to recapture my energy and health, and to follow my passion to help others reignite their lives. It was this desire that lead me to take the scary step and leave the sanctuary of the United Nations, my home for over 15 years. Saying good-bye to the guaranteed paycheck, scheduled days and external accountability to another's vision was one of my boldest moves.

The freedom I sought was REAL. What wasn't real and what I did not expect was the journey that I embarked on. I arrogantly thought, if others can then so can I after all I had an MBA, an MSc and a health coaching certification. With this backing anyone could build and run a business, or so I told myself. What no one told me was that I and I alone, not my certifications, would be my greatest asset or indeed my greatest liability.

As I ventured into the realm of entrepreneurism, the joy, enthusiasm and passion for my new venture started to wither as I came up against myself time and time again.

I came to realize the corporate realm was easy! There I was the expert, the leader and had budget, technology and a HR team at my fingertips. In this new world of entrepreneurialism, I was in uncharted waters. In business, you need to wear the hats of book keeper, marketer, sales guru etc., while still being a mom, wife, daughter and whoever else you need to be. I needed to be it all and in being it all life became the battle of me vs myself.

Lack of knowledge in the myriad of business areas fueled my insecurities and soon preconceived notions and limiting beliefs around what I was or wasn't capable of bubbled to the surface. Wow, what a ride! My once unseen flaws, to myself, now slapped me in my face at the most unexpected moments.

I did what every entrepreneur who wants to eat does, I plunged forward and pushed through. I'd have great months and then I'd stall. Sometimes for a day. I didn't call it a stall, I called it 'I need to hit the gym,' or 'I need to take my mom for lunch,' or I'd commit to something that would take my energy and concentration away from my business. Sometimes the stall extended into weeks and in those weeks I felt terrible about myself!

I told myself everything under the sun. I told myself I was lazy, I didn't know how to, if only I had money I could, I need a marketer, I need to sales team, I need this, I need that. Everything was *external* to me. I'm not saying these things aren't needed, I'm saying my self-worth was an issue. It was my inability to clear my personal self-judgment and self-incriminating beliefs about me that kept stalling me. At its core this was a self-worth issue.

I've learned in running my own business that I must address me! Having a cold hard look in the mirror has been paramount.

This includes looking at things you've told yourself that you can do and you can't do, things that others have told you about yourself that you've bought into. Look at the innocent things that someone criticized you for, or made comment on, like how you write, eat, or even speak. If you heard them and took any of their comments on as a value judgment about yourself, do yourself a favor and address them internally.

Let me tell a story to help convey what I mean.

I grew up in family where cleanliness was next to godliness and godliness was deemed to be perfection. My mother got a 10 out of 10 for housekeeping. Man, I tell you we had a perfect house it was clean all the time. And when I worked for the UN I had a nanny and housekeeper, my house was spotlessly clean.

After leaving the UN, my children and I moved to Canada, the nanny went home and I went to work for myself. My sweet husband continued to work overseas which meant, my former UN identity was completely stripped away. I was now the primary care giver, a business owner and manager and I became responsible for cleaning my own home. Talk about an eye-opening experience and life change!

You can understand being raised by my mother with her 10/10 for housecleaning, and having a cleaner for more than 10 years the value of a clean home followed me into my entrepreneurial life. So there I was doing my business and everything was going great. Then one night, my sister and I were having a little heart to heart and she says to me "Your house is a mess." I don't remember the exact words but I took it as a judgment on my ability to manage a home and on my value as a mother and a person.

Her passing comment lead to a shift in my business because I started to spend more time cleaning. In case you're wondering, cleaning, unless it's your business isn't an income producing, lead generating activity, or a networking opportunity; hell it doesn't even fall into marketing. It is necessary, the questions is, to whose standards?

I had to do some inner work to decide whose values and standards I would choose to live up to, those of family or my own. I asked myself value questions like is cleaning more important to *me* than serving clients? Is a clean home more important to *me* than helping others achieve their greatness? Through this line of thought it was easier to determine my values for a clean home fall in the range of 5-8, depending on my schedule.

This may seem inconsequential but I tell the story to share how something small can have big Impact on our business, if we let it.

The point here is deal with your stuff!!

The reality is if you want to be *more* (a better business person, mom, friend, even fitter and healthier), you have to become more. Once I did, my confidence, self-assuredness and internal awareness launched my business forward.

Moving on, the second element to build a successful business is energy. I'm talking E=Mc2 amounts of energy. There are so many thieves waiting to zap our energy and leave us crawling to the couch for just a few minutes of rest.

Nothing is more of an energy killer than feeling like you're a failure, or have no idea what you're doing, as tends to happen when you're doing tasks outside of your traditional skill set.

There's no point in beating yourself up, it doesn't help and you can't outrun the feelings.

Take a deep breath and decide to breathe through your feelings and push forward. My first blog took 14 hours to write and post. I was up till 3 am and wanted to cry because I was so frustrated at the technology. Each time I wrote one it took less time. Eventually as my competence grew and with it my confidence till the point where it became another task to do, with no emotion attached to it and no loss of sleep. Where might this competence, confidence, energy loop come into play in your business?

Focus on generating energy by removing energy thieves from your life. The five common energy thieves are:

1. Food.

2. Lack of movement.

3. Poor hydration.

4. Environmental toxins.

5. Toxic relationships, including with oneself.

Each of these areas can dramatically impact your energy and health. Have you ever experienced poor health, or exhaustion? If so, you'll know that life without energy and health leaves us walking around in a dazed haze, going to bed tired and waking up tired, it affects our memory, our mood and our business. If you look at people longing for their level of energy, it's time to do a little detoxing.

And you can! I found this detoxing step critical to recapturing my energy and building a business that I have incorporated it as a foundational element in my coaching programs, I hope it will serve you too.

There are so many stereotypes around about age and energy levels. My experience is when we challenge them and seek to understand the workings of our own body and mind we can boost our energy beyond what we thought possible. At 51, I have the energy of my twenties and thirties. I've enrolled in a gymnastics class, become a fitness instructor, and before the years out I will compete in a master's swim meet, how crazy is that? These things all fuel my self-esteem, health and my business. Imagine what it could do for you with heightened energy levels?

Finally, the third point and something to guard with vigilance is your ability to focus. Staying focused, on point and minimizing distractions has a monumental impact on business. I suffered, and still do occasionally, from the bright shinny object syndrome. Looking for the silver bullet that would skyrocket my business. It never arrived! I finally figured out that success comes from focus directed action.

I spent days in my basement writing, creating, trying to figure things out. Every time I'd gain momentum any number of things would happen. The phone rang, the dog came down, the kids came down or the parents would pop over. Each of these distractions took my attention away from building my business.

Staying focused isn't just about managing your time, it's about setting times to have things completed by and setting non-negotiable deadlines. Without which, dates risk being pushed and with it, your business success. When I schedule talks and classes no matter how busy I am I'm always there. However, leave me with a wishy washy schedule with no deadline and there's a good chance it will take 10-20 times longer to get to it, never mind complete it.

I find this brain dump exercise helps me to stay on track and focus on what I need to be doing.

1. Get a big 3M sticky note.

2. Simply place the note on your wall and write everything you have to get done on it. Be crazy write all over the paper, not in lines.

3. Group the tasks into categories. My categories include: website, product development, personal development, family, home, client outreach etc. In each category prioritize the items and set non-negotiable dates.

4. Knock off the easiest ones first. This helps you gain momentum, and holds you accountable to your own goals, which helps you feel good.

5. Ask yourself, "What's the most important thing you need to do at that moment." Then go do it.

6. Set a timer for 30 minutes, turn off all computer notifications, all phones and put a do not disturb sign on your door. Work non-stop for 30 minutes. I was amazed how long 30 minutes is when there are absolutely no distractions.

Office hours are a signal to your brain that it's time to focus. I learnt this after thinking, as an entrepreneur, I could work anytime. Setting office hours gives you self-accountability and let's your friends, family and clients know that this isn't a hobby for you.

When I set office hours, my weekends became fun again and so did my business. I lost the feeling of I should be writing, budgeting, bookkeeping or teaching. Weekends are free for self-care, non-business related activates and family connection.

While peeling back the layers of focus, I recommend spending time up front in your business to determine who your ideal clients are, when and how you'll service them. This comes from my own mistakes when I first got into business, my clients worked during the day, because of this my coaching calls were between the hours of 4:00 and 8:00 pm or early morning. These exact times were when I wanted to be seeing the kids out the door or greeting them afterschool.

My lack of ideal client planning left me disenchanted with my business and disassociated from my kids. This was not the life or business I signed up for and so back to the drawing board I went. Because I hadn't achieved my objective of being more involved with the kids, I felt like a failure in business and life. I wasn't, I'd just created a business building it around my life. When I scheduled my business around my life the stars of energy, happiness and business fulfillment came together.

This one act removed freed up more energy, removed parental guilt and set my business on a sustainable path.

My business came about to create freedom and help others recreate their lives. Freedom is a big word one that meant different things for me 18 months ago than it does now. In my first 18 months of business, I lacked freedom because I lived in my head always weighing up what I should be doing, how I should be showing up, or spending my time. The lack of scheduling lead to over committing and under delivering which made me feel less than I am myself down which affected my energy, health and happiness as a business woman and you guessed it as a woman.

In 18 months, using the techniques described in this chapter I turned my business, health and happiness around.

True freedom comes from developing simple habits that fuel your mind, body and business and addressing anything that threatens to take your focus away from them. Look in the mirror, are you the person you want to be? Is your business an integrated reflection of you or are you a slave to it, feeling trapped and beating yourself up?

I continue to walk the journey of checking in with myself, being aware of how things affect me on a cellular level and of what I'm taking on that isn't my stuff at all. Creating personal time on my calendar helps me slow life down and is critical to ongoing development of what I now call a lifestyle business. One where I am comfortable in my passion of helping others create a life that energizes them and fills them from the inside out.

These lessons are what I've learnt on my journey from professional working woman to a mom that's an entrepreneur. It's taken me awhile and lots of tears of frustration and growth, I'm sure there is more to come. My hope is my discoveries will benefit you on your journey.

In closing. Break business down the basics, ask yourself who your ideal client is, what your scheduled hours will be, what mental junk needs to be cleared out, how you can detoxify and what focus you need right now. You have within you everything you need, trust yourself to succeed.

Dana Zarcone

Dana Zarcone, known as a revolutionary leadership coach, is passionate about helping her clients live life all in and full out. She takes her clients on an exciting journey of self-discovery that allows them to step into their power and enjoy epic success in life and business. She has the pleasure of working with individuals, small companies and corporate clients, globally.

Dana has her Masters in counseling and is a national certified counselor, certified core energetics practitioner, certified life coach and energy healer. She's the founder of Source Your Joy ™ and is a motivational speaker, author and host of The Your Shift Matters podcast.

Website: www.DanaZarcone.com

Chapter 5

Source Joy for Ultimate Success

By Dana Zarcone

It was 2:30 in the morning and I was on the bathroom floor bawling my eyes out while I listened to the Whitney Houston song, 'I Look to You.' I listened to that song over and over again as I begged God to bring me home. My heart was breaking into a million pieces. I was pleading with God. I told him that I wasn't the type of person that would ever commit suicide, but I was ready to come when he'd have me. I told him that, when it was time, I'd go willingly. I wouldn't argue with his decision. I wouldn't fight him on it. I was giving up on myself. I was giving up on life. I was willing to leave my kids behind so that I wouldn't have to suffer anymore. So they wouldn't have to see their mother fail, yet again.

I had hit my personal rock bottom. At the time I felt like a huge failure. I didn't know who I was anymore. Life had gotten the best of me. I had become someone I didn't recognize. Who was I? How on earth did I get here?!

Over the years, I did everything that was expected of me. I went to college, spent 24 years climbing the corporate ladder. I worked my way up to senior leadership, running large, global multi-million dollar projects and managing large organizations. By most people's standards, I was really successful.

I had a life that I had only dared to dream of. I drove a fancy car, lived in a big house, traveled the world ... but it wasn't enough. I wasn't happy. In fact, I was stressed, depressed and unfulfilled. I knew, deep in my heart, that I was meant to do something more with my life. Life had bigger plans for me and I knew it! So, how on earth did I end up having a breakdown in the middle of the night on a cold bathroom floor?

Drum roll please. I became an entrepreneur. Sounds crazy, doesn't it? But it's true.

I've always had a passion for helping people. I've always been a self-proclaimed 'personal development junkie.' So, I decided the right path for me was to become a counselor. While I was still working, I went back to school and got my Masters in Counseling, specializing in domestic abuse. Just a month later, I graduated from a four-year program at the Institute of Core Energetics in New York and got certified as a core energetics practitioner.

For a few years. I double dipped. I worked during the day and saw clients at night. Eventually, I decided to take a leap of faith, leave corporate America and work with clients full time. I mean, after all, how hard could it be? I was an accomplished senior leader in the corporate world. I had vast experience in sales, marketing, operations, financial management, etc. so I could easily leverage my background as an entrepreneur, right?! You'd think so, but it wasn't that easy.

When I decided to take a leap of faith, I jumped off the corporate ladder and, as I like to describe it, I landed in quicksand while wearing a straitjacket! I had underestimated how tough it would be to start my own business. I struggled for years as the quicksand got deeper, the straitjacket got tighter. In essence, I didn't have a business at all. I had a really expensive hobby. I was the captain of my own sinking ship, getting deeper and deeper in debt and going nowhere fast.

I was desperate to make this work, so I chased shiny objects, buying program after program. I'd sign up for free webinars and once the sales pitch came, I whipped out my wallet, convinced that *this* program was the answer. Unlike all the other programs I've bought before, this one was *the* one that was going to make me successful.

Wrong!

They didn't make me successful. Heck, I don't even think I finished any of them!

So, how is it that someone so successful in the corporate world could be an utter failure as an entrepreneur?

I didn't know who I really I was. I wasn't connected to a 'big why' that would keep me motivated when things got tough. I wasn't aligned with my passion and purpose in life.

I didn't know it at the time but, for over 24 years, my identity was directly linked to my job title, my paycheck, and the next big promotion. Obviously, I was not my job title or the position that I held. I was so much more than that, but that's not how I saw it at the time. I was proud of my accomplishments and, looking back, I now know those accomplishments were how I showed the world I was worthwhile loving.

My success in the corporate world was not mine alone. It was the culmination of the leaders that I followed and the teams that I lead. My success was the result of having resources and infrastructure that I could easily tap into. In some ways, my success was the result of what was 'out there.'

Being an entrepreneur was different. My success hinged on me and me alone. There is no 'out there' – there's just me. I didn't have other resources and infrastructure to can tap into. I was now the chief financial officer, the marketing director, the sales executive, the administrative assistant and the operations manager. Me and me alone.

You see, being an entrepreneur isn't all that it's cracked up to be. If you hang out in the entrepreneur space at all, you'll hear a lot of people talking about the thousands of dollars they make "while they sleep." You'll read stories of people going from zero to six figures in a matter of months. While some people's stories are legitimate, most of them are hogwash.

The truth is, being an entrepreneur has been the most difficult, yet most rewarding thing I've ever done! To be successful, I had to get real with myself so I could get out of my own way. I had to dance with my demons, grapple with the gremlins and reconnect with my higher self. In doing so, I learned a lot about myself, about others and about life.

So, what lessons did I learn? What advice would I give you?

Obviously, as you've read already, my advice doesn't include looking 'out there.' My advice won't be the tactical things like 'build a solid marketing plan' or 'clearly define your prospect.' While those are important, they won't matter if you don't have your shit together. So, it's about focusing inside yourself, getting real with yourself and connecting with who you really are as a person and what you're truly meant to do in this lifetime. So how do you do this?

By sourcing your joy!

As the founder of Source Your Joy, I've developed a process that, conveniently enough, leverages the acronym ... source joy. It's represents a path that leads away from all the 'noise' and onto a journey of self-exploration and self-discovery. This path leads you to a place where you are sure to succeed!

Set Your Intent and Willingness to Succeed

Being an entrepreneur is really, really hard. It takes drive, determination and a lot of perseverance. It requires you to dig deep within yourself and know exactly why you want to build your own business. If your primary goal is to have a flexible schedule, make good money and spend more time with your kids, you're in for a rude awakening! Being an entrepreneur means working more hours than you've ever worked before, spending less time with your kids (and feeling really guilty about it!) and making way less than minimum wage ... at least initially. And, that's just being an entrepreneur ... not even a successful one!

You need to go into entrepreneurship with your eyes wide open. Know that, at first, you'll have to make a lot of sacrifices and be willing to put in the work – no matter what! Be willing to do whatever it takes to be successful.

Own and Face Your Fear

Fear is a paralyzing emotion. Whether we're conscious of it or not, we all live in fear. We fear failure, life, death, loving, being loved, being hurt, rejected, abandoned - you name it – we fear it. However, interestingly enough, what I've learned through my own process, and working with my clients, is that we also fear success. It seems counterintuitive doesn't it? But, I see it all the time.

Why might you fear success? You fear success because you fear the unknown. You fear success because in doing so, you can't hide behind your stories anymore. Becoming successful means pushing through the resistance. It means you have to stand up tall and claim your rightful place in this world. Which means you have to be willing to be seen, to be vulnerable. Being vulnerable means you might experience what you desperately want to avoid – the pain of being rejected, abandoned, unloved, or judged.

You fear success because it means you have to show up and claim your power in a real way. You fear owning all of who you really are because it threatens those around you. Do you have a fear of success?

You know you have a fear of success if you:

- Procrastinate all the time.

- Don't finish what you started.

- Blame everything and everybody else for your lack of progress.

- Are easily distracted.

- Second guess yourself.

- Get close to a breakthrough and something goes terribly wrong.

Do you see yourself in any of these statements?

Now, don't get me wrong. It's not that you don't want to be successful. Of course you do! However, if you're working really hard and not moving the needle – getting nowhere fast – then there's a part of you that fears success. Own it, face it, and work through it so it doesn't have power over you anymore.

Uncover Confidence Zappers

So what are confidence zappers?

They're misperceptions or limiting beliefs you have about yourself and the world around you that you learned from someone, or something, else that you bought into as your truth!

The reality is that your life isn't a struggle because you lack confidence. You lack confidence because your life's been a struggle!

You, my friend, are a wounded warrior. As a child, you've experienced pain, rejection, abandonment, and criticism. You've been reprimanded, punished, and shut down by someone close to you. As a result, you've developed some misperceptions, or limiting beliefs about yourself such as 'I'm not lovable,' 'I'm not good enough,' 'I'll never be successful,' 'I suck at _____ (fill in the blank).'

You're not conscious of most of them, but you bought into this mumbo jumbo very early on in life. As a result, you approach life with a faulty belief system and you'll focus on trying to prove that your faulty beliefs and misperceptions are indeed valid.

This validation process will keep you stuck. As they say, 'you reap what you sow.' If you feel you don't deserve to be successful, you won't be! When confidence zappers are at play, it's going to be really tough to build a successful business. As a result, it's important to uncover your confidence zappers and dispel them.

The confidence you need to build a business is developed over time. It's a process. You gain confidence through experience and in order to get that experience you have to go out of your comfort zone and do things you've probably never done before. This will bring up the fear we discussed earlier. So what you need at this point is courage. The kind of courage that allows you to face your fear, honor your intent and willingness to succeed, and push ahead.

Recognize Your Resistance

When you decide to embark on entrepreneurship, there's usually a part of you that doesn't want to rock the boat. The part of you that prefers the status quo. That part of you is your crew member named 'resistance.'

As you're going about your day, notice if you find yourself holding your breath, tensing up, or feeling 'sea sick.' As an entrepreneur, it's easy to get overwhelmed and stressed out. If this happens, simply breathe and ask yourself: 'in this moment, what is true and right for me?' As you become more conscious, more aware, and more intuitive you'll begin to align more with your truth.

Realize that as you embark on your journey of entrepreneurship, you're bound to go against the tide from time to time. You'll feel the resistance and, just like the tides, this is completely natural. With that said, it's important to know when you're not just going against the tide and there's a huge storm approaching. If you feel you're about to go into a storm, this should be a sign for you to take a closer look. It usually means that your ship's defense system, or ego, is being challenged and the crew member named 'Resistance' doesn't want to change. So that's when it's time to sound the alarms, turn on your navigation lights and look for the light house that's just up ahead.

Trust that you're not about to run a-ground and that eventually, you'll find smooth waters again if you just follow your conscious intuition. To be a good captain, you need to practice and gain real life experience. Each time you leave the dock, you'll get more experience on how to steer the ship based on the conditions. You'll become intuitive on how to navigate during a big storm, how to approach the big waves and deal with the tides. You'll learn how to do all of this and still ensure a smooth ride, in spite of the rough waters. Your intuition will lead the way.

Cultivate Compassion

I'm sure you're compassionate towards others. However, are you compassionate towards yourself? I find that most people have a hard time with this. Most entrepreneurs I know are perfectionists. Instead of celebrating even the smallest successes, they focus on the failures. As entrepreneurs, I find that we are really hard on ourselves.

I have two words for you: stop it!

Stop focusing on the woulda, coulda, shoulda's. Stop focusing on all the things that should have gotten done, decisions you could have made, things you would have done differently. Stop 'shoulding' on yourself!

Don't be so hard on yourself. Give yourself a break. Practice self-compassion. Building a business is really tough. You don't have to make it harder by brow beating yourself. Instead, focus on all of the little successes and, eventually, the little successes turn into big successes and you're well on your way to building a successful business.

Embrace a Higher Power

You're more than what you appear to be. The law of antinomy says that you're both human and divine, not one or the other. It's my opinion that the goal is to awaken and become a balanced, unified, spiritual being. To do this, you need to be completely responsible for, and consciously participate in, your own personal journey.

You should become a conscious co-creator of your business by embracing a higher power. Turn inward in search of your truth. When you find your truth, honor it wholeheartedly because when you choose to live in your truth, you will assume an active role in your divine plan.

Invite a higher power to support you on your journey. When you invite spirit in, it's from a place of strength and it will unlock your greatest potential. As spiritual beings, it's important to connect to, and crave, a deeper connection to your divine self. By doing so, together, you can create great opportunities for yourself and receive universal guidance and support along the way.

Join a Universal Consciousness

Everything in our entire universe is made up of one cosmic substance. You're made up of energy and atoms. In human anatomy, cells expand and contract as do individual organs such as the heart and lungs. You're made of energy and the movement of that energy is your life force.

You can tap into that life force and increase your capacity for a higher level of consciousness that is innate in all of us. By connecting to your own spiritual essence, and developing a higher level of consciousness, you can bring more attention, awareness and energy into being fully present with yourself.

When you're fully present, you're more aligned with your truth. This, in turn, helps you align with your intent and willingness to do what it takes to succeed, let go of the fear and resistance and resolve your confidence zappers. See, it's all starting to come together, isn't it!?

The truth is we're all yearning for a higher state of consciousness. We're all meant to find our way back to the source. We all want to be whole and to live our lives aligned with our passion and purpose. Ultimately, that's why we become entrepreneurs in the first place! And what I am proposing here is if you embody spirit and do your inner work, you will be able to show up in your business, and in life, wholeheartedly and unapologetically. You will be clear on what your 'why' is and you won't waver.

Observe Universal Laws

While the Law of Attraction is all the craze these days, there are many other universal laws that are working in concert to manifest things in your life. Edgar Cayce was one of the most studied psychics of our time. He would give readings that talked about universal laws – the basic laws by which the world operates. In his readings, he talks about how the proper use of these laws affect our lives, our relationships and the quality of both.

I won't get into these laws now because that is not the purpose of this chapter. However, suffice it to say that these laws work together like the instruments of an orchestra, creating the symphony of life. If you take some time to understand and apply these laws, they can have a huge impact on your life and your business.

Yearn for Something More

If you don't yearn for something more in your life, you won't live your life all in and full out. If you don't aim high and set big, bold goals for your business, you'll never reach your highest potential. You, my friend, have unlimited potential and you can tap into the infinite possibilities that are waiting for you. The key is to find that spark in you that wants to be aligned with your passion and purpose, connected to truth, and in relationship with your higher self, spirit, and a universal consciousness.

You have the capability of living a life that, up to this point, you've only dared to dream of. Don't settle for a life that doesn't excite you. Instead, be committed to living your life all in and full out, then grab the bull by the horns and go for it!

Remember, life is a journey not a destination. If you yearn for something more, you'll stretch yourself and make things happen in your life. You'll be able to approach life with a healthy curiosity that will open up a whole new world of opportunities for you.

As I stated earlier, I feel very strongly that everything starts from within and manifests out into your life. The struggles that you have, the challenges and successes you experience, are because of you. You reap what you sow. As a result, I encourage you to start within and work your way out.

These strategies are meant to stir your soul. They're meant to challenge the ego self that has served you up until now – the ego self that is unable to propel you past your discontent, barriers and obstacles and into a state of peace, love and joy and, ultimately, success!

It's time to awaken your soul so you can begin to connect to the craving you have for a life with higher purpose and deeper meaning. A life where you're connected to your divine self, your true identity – an integrated sate of being. Synthesize all aspects of yourself – mind, body, heart and soul – so that you can build a successful business, be ecstatically happy in your life and, ultimately, source your joy.

DeeAnne Riendeau

DeeAnne Riendeau is changing the world, one powerful idea after another. The visionary behind 'Your Holistic Earth,' the first comprehensive holistic healthcare network in Canada, DeeAnne has been nominated for countless awards.

Profoundly affected by a near-death experience in an early life fraught with chronic illness, DeeAnne rebounded with the courageous drive and determination that led to her health administration degree and saw her through an impressively diverse healthcare career.

A popular speaker, author and radio host, DeeAnne imbues everything she does with tenacity and positive energy, especially her quest to make alternative healthcare more accessible and affordable.

Website: https://www.yourholisticearth.ca/

Facebook: https://www.facebook.com/yourholisticearth/

Twitter: https://twitter.com/urholisticearth

Chapter 6

Your Business Has a Pulse

By DeeAnne Riendeau

When I was a candy loving five-year-old, something out of this world happened to me. As I enjoyed a jawbreaker: hard and round, I tried to speak and when I took a breath in, the candy lodged in my throat. I choked. I struggled to catch my breath as my parents ran towards me. My dad came behind me, wrapped his arms around my waist and began to heave back. He thrust with all his might trying to get the candy out. I felt my feet lift from the floor with each thrust. The pressure was intense. As he and I both continued to struggle, I went limp in his arms. In this moment I had an out of body experience. I now hovered above my parents as I watched them in panic below. My mom was now running to the phone to call for help and my dad was trying to use his fingers to pry the candy out. As I floated above them I felt...*peace*. It was a calm and a knowing of what life was *really* about.

With me limp on the floor, in desperation my dad used his thumb and was able to pop the candy out. Within a few seconds, I rushed back into my body and I gasped as life was brought back to my physical self. What a feeling it was to breathe again. The emotional, spiritual and mental impacts of this experience would change me for life.

At five, I knew that I had profound missions to fulfill. I made the decision right then that I would *not* waste a second of my life. I made the choice to live my life to the fullest.

Fast forward to now and I reflect on how much I have experienced: fifteen years of health care, over ten certificates, diplomas and degrees, seven years of volunteerism, five businesses all the while living a full family life with a husband and two beautiful children just to name a few. I have not wasted a moment. We all have a life purpose. We all have missions to fulfill. It's critical you uncover yours if you want to have success on all levels.

Relationships, personal wellbeing and businesses will be much richer if you pursue your dreams and visions and set out to serve the highest good. I have grown to know that true power in all business is ensuring you honour the heart and soul of the business. Treat your business as a living breathing entity. Treating your business as such will allow you to better align with your business to ensure that it is fulfilling your mission. This is the ultimate destination in each of our personal lives, to carry out our life's purpose.

This chapter will explore the three parts of your business as a living breathing entity. We will discuss the heart of your business, which is your why, the breath of your business which is your day to day action and the soul of your business which are your values, core beliefs and attributes. The goal of reading this chapter is to create a paradigm shift in how you see and treat your business which will ultimately help you to expand and grow your business like never before!

The Heart of Business

You are the heart of your business. You saw an opportunity or had a vision and it became so important to you that you pursued it and made it come to life. Understanding *why* you are running the business is a critical and core piece of your business success. If you don't understand your why…then your passion, motivation and zest for your business will fade quickly and the clients that you want to connect with will have a hard time relating and buying into whatever it is you are selling or offering.

I want to start by sharing my why because it will help you to get the best idea of your own why. Understanding and sharing your why has become a more powerful business strategy than ever before as people shift to a more social and emotional view of relating to each other.

Here is my why:

I was born sick. My mom and dad had me in and out of doctors' offices and on numerous medications for the majority of the first few years of life. By the time I was five years old the doctors knew that something more drastic needed to be done and so I underwent surgery to remove my tonsils. The hope was that this would make me well and end the constant burden of my illnesses. But alas, my body was not strong enough to fight off the numerous bugs that would go around from year to year and I continued to spend a lot of time being unwell, resting in bed, eating chicken noodle soup and popsicles.

Despite being sick, feeling weak and feeling like I would miss out I didn't feel sorry for myself. Instead I took full advantage of life when I was well. After my near death experience, I decided that nothing would stop me from pursuing my destiny. Certainly not being sick.

The illness and the near death experience allowed me to have a better understanding of life. I knew the fragility of each and every soul and I also knew the incredible purpose we all have. As a result of my childhood experiences, I gained some incredible gifts. One of which is that I am highly empathic and can sense energy. Another was my trust in my intuition.

Due to my heightened empathic abilities and my strong desire to serve others, I chose a career in health care. I became an emergency medical technician, a dental assistant, an instructor in both of those fields and a health business owner several times over. However, as I continued on my journey I still struggled with chronic illness. Diagnoses of irritable bowel syndrome and fibromyalgia in my twenties were in fact blessings because I had learned that life didn't happen to me but life happened for me. To teach me, grow me and guide me along my path which leads directly to my life purpose. I chose to live my life so fully that I decided to make a choice about my health. I decided that I would not be defined by illness. I would overcome the challenge even if I had to ask for help.

I sought holistic health care to help me overcome a weakened immune system and aching body. It was in this journey that I realized there was very little support for those seeking holistic health care. There was no alternative health care system in existence. No place where people could go to find guided and loving support when they needed it the most. I tried so many things and spent so much money, time and energy trying to get help. It is no wonder people just give up or continue to use the current system we know of treating the symptoms. I was lucky, I found the right help for me but I knew there had to be a better way. This was the beginning of my vision, the first holistic health care system in Canada. This is a place where people can discover resources, services and products to enhance their well-being, reduce their suffering, and have the best quality of life possible. Are you ready to live better?

What do you think of my story? Do you feel like you are more connected to me? Would you want to work with me? Or at least get to know me better?

Your why is so critical to your business because it is what connects you emotionally to your clients. Sure you can do business without a why but wow does it ever shift your business once you know, understand and share your why. It is after all, the heart of your business.

As a business owner your why should be a significant part of your business. Use your why in your marketing and communication with others and it will set you apart. Knowing your why ensures you stay on track, attract the right clients and helps to define your boundaries so that you can stay in alignment with your purpose. Understanding and sharing your why enables you to use it to connect and strengthen your relationships. Your why is a fundamental piece to ensure you have success in your business.

Your why does not need to be related to a trauma near death or some crazy epiphany. Your why can be simple but you need to know, understand and share it!

"You can only become truly accomplished at something you love. Don't make money your goal. Instead pursue the things you love doing, and then do them so well that people can't take their eyes off of you."

- Maya Angelou

The Breath of Businesses

You breathe for your businesses and therefore must consider yourself the lungs of the business. This means that you must treat your business as such. It cannot survive if you do not live it and breathe it constantly. Here are my top 10 ways to live and breathe your business so that you come out on top:

1. Think about your business often.

2. Connect with, and listen to your business.

3. Write out your action items, goals and expectations.

4. See the opportunities and treat every activity, whether non business related or not, as an opportunity to connect and build relationships in which you can serve others.

5. Network like crazy. Build relationships consistently for clients but also for collaboration and partnership by finding out what they need.

6. When you don't feel like it, you do it anyway. Stop making excuses.

7. Learn all ways, grow all ways, nurture all ways.

8. Invest in you and your business.

9. Adapt when required.

10. Take action.

I think about my business all the time, almost. Driving in my car, lying in bed, even while tucking my kids in (insert guilty sigh here). Sometimes the best come at the most inopportune times but I take them in anyway. This means that it is a common theme, it becomes part of me and I become part of it. You have to constantly think of ways to enhance your business. Your thoughts are so potent that when you start to vision where your business is going and what you want it to be, you begin the manifestation process.

Using thought to manifest your life purpose can take you far but something that can help you go even farther in your business is to start having conversations with your business. Try to listen to what your business wants just like you listen to your own intuition. The more you listen the more you will hear. It will help you gain clarity and ensure you are aligning with your purpose.

It's critical that when you think about your business and when you listen to your business that you write the information down. Even if it doesn't make sense at the time, write it all out. Not only will this help you ground and focus so the information's not bouncing around in your head all the time but it also assists with manifesting the ideas energetically. Writing thoughts and ideas that come to you will help you to create an even clearer plan. This can be in the form of a business plan, which every business should have, but I suggest you take it even further by having a journal that you take wherever you go so you can write those magnificent ideas and thoughts down no matter where you are. Plans *will* change overtime especially if you are adapting as you should be so this is a continuous process in every business.

Every time you go out, there are potential opportunities for you to build a relationship. The grocery store line, the kids' soccer practice, church! Every individual is a potential client, partner, sponsor, friend, etc. Setting the intention that you are going to meet and connect with someone new is one of the best intentions to set each day for your business. Relationships are such a fundamental piece because they give your business breath. Relationships lead to opportunities that lead to clients which leads to revenue. Without relationships we have no business.

A key in building trust and respect is helping to support whatever that persons needs are. Perhaps they need a good mechanic and you happen to know one. Help them and typically that comes back tenfold. I had met with a potential client and she just wasn't ready to commit to my program. So instead, I shared her Facebook posts and championed for her anyway. It took a year but she became a client. When we nurture relationships we in turn nourish our business. Opportunities are everywhere and are endless. Seek them out. Make yourself aware of them.

Business owners have to network consistently. It is the best way to build the relationships you want for your business. I recommend once per week minimum with formal networking and 1-3 times per week of non-formal networking (I.E. church, volunteer board). Although some people may not be ideal clients, they could be a great referral source, collaborator or supporter of you don't be too hasty when prequalifying your leads for your business. It is important to understand who you are speaking to and uncover what *they* need so you in turn can get them what they need if possible. By allowing the person you are speaking with to share as much as possible with you, you are able to determine the type of fit for your business and whether or not you should pursue them or move on to the next person.

Some days I just don't feel like doing it. Some days I just want to stay in bed too. You must ask yourself this question: Is it because you are lazy or making excuses out of fear (which we discuss in the following section) or is it because you truly need to rest? If it's the latter then, yes, rest up because you are going to need the fuel to keep going. However, if it's just an excuse to stay stuck then get yourself moving! You can make all the excuses in the world for yourself if you want but do you want to be stuck in excuse mode or do you want to take action?

Ensure you stay moving forward by filling your own personal cup. This means continuing your own education and self-care. Learn, grow and nurture your own self so you are at your best for your business. Since you are such a fundamental aspect to ensuring your business lives, you must be sure to honour yourself. Business owners who take poor care of themselves often lack care of their business.

Investing in yourself by taking care of yourself and investing in your business to allow it to grow go hand in hand. They are both worthy investments and are critical. Business start up and growth require money. It is just the way it is. Be prepared to invest a fair amount of money and time in your business. Be smart about where you put your money but be prepared for the business to cost more than what you perhaps anticipated. Here is an example. I went through four revisions of my website because I was too afraid to spend a lot of money upfront. Ironically, I spent just as much money as I would have to have it done right the first time and I would have been much less stressed. Invest the money to do things right but always negotiate!

You and your business must always be willing to adapt. It is the survival of the fittest and you better be prepared to make changes if you want to take your business all the way. As technology races by, we are constantly faced with newer, faster and better. You must have some foresight as to what is coming and be ready for customer demands so you can fulfil their needs always.

Take action. When you set your intentions and your write out your goals then follow through in order to manifest the business you dream of. Joel A Barker says *"Vision without action is merely a dream. Action without vision just passes the time. Vision with action can change the world."*

In taking action we breathe for our company and the business can thrive.

The Soul of Business

Your values, core beliefs and attributes all contribute to the type of energy your business has. The soul is the underlying energy of the business. What type of energy are you putting into your business? It is common that when your business has momentum, you can feel the energy of it and you, in turn get energy personally from that. You should feed your business vitality and in turn it gives you energy! Whether the energy is positive or negative is up to you.

The reality is that if we are truly doing what we are meant to do, our life's purpose, then courage and all the other qualities you must possess start to come naturally. They become part of the energy of the company as the business starts to take on what you put in. Our personal soul assists us to keep us on our path to fulfill our purpose. Similarly, your businesses soul is there to do the same for your business and therefore for you.

The soul also helps you to overcome fears and obstacles. In this world we as people are trained to be a certain way. I refer to it as being put in a box. This box can limit you if you allow it to. It can be pretty comfortable in there but the truth is that this so called safe box also limits you. It stops you from living the most fulfilling life possible. The strength of your soul will push through the glass ceiling or past the perceived barriers you come to face so that you can continue to grow your business and yourself. Push yourself beyond your fears and barriers. Life is far richer when you do.

"Often the difference between a successful person and a failure is not one has better abilities or ideas, but the courage that one has to bet on one's ideas, to take a calculated risk--and to act."

--Andre Malraux

Your business is a living breathing entity. Treat it with love and respect. Honour the heart, breath and soul of your business and you will have a full and prosperous life in all ways.

Dorothy Briggs

Dorothy Briggs is a vibrant, dynamic leader who has become an undeniable catalyst for women, effectively connecting and collaborating for the greater good. Gifted with an ardent entrepreneurial spirit, Dorothy has received endless accolades for her accomplishments as the founder and publisher of Womanition® Magazine, a venture so successful that it led to an entire network of Womanition Connect Groups.

Ms. Briggs continues to educate, motivate, and inspire business women, honing talent through the thriving Womanition Mentorship Program, Womanition BizBrigade Leadership Conference, and offering a program of recognition and celebration with Womanition SuPEARLative Awards.

Website: www.womanition.com

http://www.womanition.com/wiki/MentorshipProgram

http://www.womanition.com/wiki/SupearlativeAwards

Chapter 7

From All the B.S. to
Business Success

By Dorothy Briggs

I have it seen it all, when it comes to business B.S. Actually, no, I have *lived* it! Hell, let's talk B.S. in general. It seemed to be my only lot in life at certain times, but I have survived! I have lived to tell this tale.

I knew I was different from the rest of my family by the time I reached my early teens. It took me a lot longer to realize what the real difference actually was. Now I revel in it! Why? Because It has propelled me on through any and all adversity to create my current empire, 'Womanition,' a multi-faceted venture committed to uniting, educating, supporting and promoting business 'womanpower.' Yes, the difference was that I had ambition.

Ambition, yes, but not much direction in those early years, although I never hesitated to explore new horizons. I have waitressed, modelled, managed companies, scooped ice cream, and shampooed hair. No one could fault my versatility! I have worked in ladies clothing at a Woolco department store and I have sold panty-hose from the back of a white VW van. At one point, I even had my own carpet cleaning business!

Not overly inspired by high school studies, my focus was on extra-curricular activities like my 'dream man,' my first love, who became my husband and then, subsequently, my ex-husband all before I turned the tender age of 23. I may have been young, but I was the only adult in that relationship and, of course, in retrospect, I realize now, in catering to his every whim, doing everything for him right down to thinking, I was giving all MY power away.

Man-o-man could I pick 'em! Ten years later, married again to another guy that was just my type: tall, dark and dashing, until I found out it was more 'tall tale telling,' drug addicted and dastardly. The marriage counsellor I consulted told me to wait a year, and fix myself first. Fix *myself!* What the hell!? As the months wore on, I came to understand what she meant. It was a very difficult time but I faithfully followed her advice even though I usually burst into tears every time I looked in the mirror at the sad, sorry woman who was losing another husband. Finally, I stopped my grieving, seized control of my life and lost 220 pounds. Yes! When I dumped his lying, cheating, alcoholic *ASS*ociation!

Fortunately, I caught myself before I was three times unlucky in love. I could see the writing on the wall in how controlling my next marital candidate could be, so much so that I actually moved away.

After three weeks, he came to visit and absence had not made my heart grow fonder, as they say. In fact, I instantly recognized how childish and ignorant he truly was and when he proposed, I refused.

Looking back, I regret not attending university as I realize now that, instead of failing at marriage, I could have been very successful at a career in my main area of interest, the law. Preferably, divorce! At the time, however, I was more psychologically focused pondering why was I always attracting these toxic types of men. As is often the case, my childhood experiences held the answer. The first man I married was so like my mother, while the second one was my definitely father all over again. We do live what we learn!

Growing up, I remember that my mother was ever vigilant about outside appearances, worrying about how we would look to others, while constantly taking steps to clean up my alcoholic father's inadvertent messes, so as to save our so called 'family reputation.' Although, financially, we were moderately well off, any extra funds went to placating the victims of my father's drunken 'accidents,' paying off the people whose cars he had damaged, whose trees he continued to mow down and whose yards he destroyed on a regular basis.

The neighbors weren't the only ones living in fear of his out of control behavior. Totally terrified, my siblings and I would literally hide when he returned home from a boozy Saturday afternoon. I remember huddling in a closet, holding my hand over my little sister's mouth, so he wouldn't find us and invent a reason to beat me for some imagined offence.

Our family ended up poverty stricken, when my father finally left us, but mercifully, we were at peace. With my mother working full time to make ends meet, though, we were now left alone to fend for ourselves. The only saving grace in it all, in my opinion, the one thing that salvaged most of our family was that my mother showed so much love towards us as little children.

Consequently, the majority of us are now thriving, prosperous adults.

The second oldest of eight, I have distanced myself, over time, from certain family members allowed to continue in their dysfunctional behavior by their own enabling loved ones. Having made the choice to surround myself with only supportive, empowering individuals for my own mental health and well-being, I do miss out on many family functions but, again, why willingly subject yourself to even more B.S.!? I know now that I deserve so much more.

I hadn't the slightest idea, at the time my second marriage was becoming a distant memory, that I would soon be introduced to my own true love in life: magazine publishing! Our attachment began innocently enough when I decided to work for a longtime girlfriend who published *Builder/Architect*, a magazine profiling the building and trades professions, showcasing their work in photos of interiors and exteriors of homes. Soon I knew every builder and tradesperson in Calgary, the city where I was living at the time. I just adored it!

The only thing missing in my happy, satisfying life was the deep connection I have always had with my mother, who was now getting up there in age, a compelling enough reason to send me back to Edmonton, the place I consider home.

As fate would have it, a week before I left, I received a call from the owner of a health and wellness magazine proposing that I buy a licensing agreement to publish in the Greater Edmonton area. Explaining that I was through with magazines, I refused, but, after much convincing, I agreed to meet her for lunch. As soon as I saw the magazine, I was absolutely smitten.

I just had to buy it, but with my previous business connections in Edmonton having long dissipated, I had to come up with new ways to build a successful support system. Hmm, what to do?

I became an unstoppable networking dynamo, attending business related events, and mixers almost every day of the week. A health and wellness trade show was a fantastic kick start. You really have to keep alert for every opportunity at this stage of new business growth. Anywhere there were people gathered for networking purposes, I made sure I was there as well. Almost five years later, I sold that health and wellness magazine back to the same woman for 1100% of what I originally paid.

Naturally, I was thrilled! The most exciting part of the whole experience, however, was that it was actually the catalyst for Womanition. Filling pages in my health and wellness magazine obviously required me to keep on coming up with innovative ideas, one of which was the concept of profiling different women in the field, much like I had done with the construction and trade professionals in the builder/architect magazine. When I implemented this in my new magazine, it worked beautifully and for the first time I felt my journey to success had truly begun!

It was a rocky road in the beginning thanks to one bitter, disgruntled woman who rallied some others around to personally attack me while trying to discredit my brand new publication all over some imagined slight.

I was devastated, especially with the extreme amount of hard work I had put into promoting these women citywide. Instead of appreciation on their part, my efforts were met with insults and scorn. My precious newly born magazine labelled a 'cheap catalogue,' a 'glorified brochure!' I actually had to hire a lawyer to forcefully persuade the ring leader to cease and desist with her slander.

Success truly is the best revenge. Eventually, the main instigator emailed me to apologize, trying to excuse her abominable behavior as just part of her natural 'feistiness' and 'piss and vinegar.' I made her face up to her bullying and told her I would forgive her once she paid her bill!

Naturally, I have let go of this unfortunate incident long ago and now, ten years later, I am so very proud of the connections I've made, the lifelong friendships I have built, and I sincerely love all my girls.

Womanition Magazine has grown to become an annual, multiple award-winning publication designed to showcase and promote women in business, providing a place for them to tell their stories, and to introduce their products and services to a new market; each page a rewarding investment for the participant. Every year a new theme is chosen for the content, the look and the layout. Anticipation builds as readers and featured entrepreneurs alike wait for the publication to reach the displays.

I host an honorary luncheon when the magazine is launched every September, where everyone involved gets together to meet each other, and spend the afternoon networking. Having realized the power of the publication to raise professional credibility, successful 'veterans' share their experiences demonstrating how they attract more customers and increase revenues using the magazine as a promotional tool. The featured professions therein enjoy partial exclusivity, creating a more diverse internal community, as well as, a much more interesting read for the public.

Once *Womanition Magazine* started to thrive, I began to see more and more opportunities to help women entrepreneurs in every aspect of their business. The truth is that people only buy from who they know, like and trust so, with the social component of the annual luncheon being so successful, I decided to expand Womanition into monthly networking meetings to facilitate long term relationship building among our members. The expansion met with rave reviews and now the networking groups are currently five strong and still growing, four interspersed in and around the Greater Edmonton area, and one thus far in Calgary.

Another extremely popular addition to the Womanition empire is the BizBrigade Leadership Conference held twice a year. A venture now five years in the running, this daylong event is a veritable business mecca for 200 plus women entrepreneurs keen on learning from the varied experts in the speaker roles, as well as conducting lucrative transactions with their fellow participants, all together in the amount of hundreds of thousands of dollars.

The concept of 'mentoring,' so essential to women new to the entrepreneurial world, was another need I wanted to fulfill for my members to help them to not only grow their business but to grow to better understand themselves. I gathered together all my 'veterans' and trusted supporters and made the case, asking would they be willing to volunteer their time and expertise. Fast forward four years and we now have a brilliant program that sells out every time, catering not just to business startups but to any businesswoman wishing to brush up on her knowledge, re-invent her marketing approach or just get a different outlook on their objectives.

The program testimonials speak volumes! Having witnessed the example set by their mentors who show up, educate, give so generously out of the goodness of their hearts, these protégés have really developed into superlative human beings with a better understanding of themselves and what it takes to achieve their goals. In fact, some of our first 'graduates' of the program are currently mentors now, themselves. Every year I am so honored to be around these amazing women who honestly care so much about these aspiring entrepreneurs and their professional success.

Just last year, in fact, I devised an informative Womanition mentorship e-course perfect for those unable to regularly attend the meetings but who are still eager to expand on their skills and knowledge. Our book, *Mentoring Women Leaders*, marketed through Amazon, is a collection of personal stories, business insights, and advice from the leaders of our Womanition community.

The more I enjoyed watching the personal and professional development of so many incredible women, the more I wanted to find some special way to honor their diligent efforts and diverse expertise. Thus my Su*PEARL*ative awards program came into being, celebrating women entrepreneurs who are 'pearls' in their profession.

In nature, a pearl starts as a foreign particle but, over time, it becomes surrounded by concentrated layers of crystalline aragonite creating those unique and valuable gemstones admired for their luster and iridescence. What a perfect metaphor for female entrepreneurs!

Like the small particle that begins a pearl, they start out with a will to succeed and then create their persona through the many layers of experiences and skills they amass. Much in the same way we marvel at nature's accomplishment of that miraculous pearl, we can recognize the evolution of an individual as they grow and come into their own unique power. That is the inspiring philosophy behind our Su*PEARL*ative awards.

My latest venture, a non-profit organization called ACES, standing for Association of a Community Engaged in Sharing has the mandate to aid in ending homelessness while creating equality, allowing indigent women and children to thrive independently. Our objective is to build an integrated, socially cohesive society by facilitating positive interaction among different communities, cultural, ethnic and religious, province wide, as well as country wide.

I have always felt a strong connection to immigrant women, the humble sweetness I have found in them, and their willingness to share. I can only imagine what it must be like, new to a country facing immense language barriers, feeling alone, not knowing a soul, yet having to face the fear of being judged as an outsider while you strive to fit in. I want to reach out and mentor these courageous women, to teach and help them in every way possible to facilitate their assimilation to Canadian life. I sincerely believe in fairness for everyone. The color of someone's skin is irrelevant. If people are sincere and they need a break, I'll give them one if I'm able.

My early dysfunctional background has taught me many lessons, but, predominately, what it feels like to have no control. Yet my having survived, despite all the negative feelings, actions and events, is what gives me the most self-pride. I know now that the only person I want or need to impress is myself.

Yes, it can be overwhelming, even terrifying being out there on your own following your heart, facing the subsequent challenges and trying new things. The big scary question is always, "What if I fail?" Well, what if you do fail? I tell myself, "It's only money." If I lose money, I am confident in my ability to make even more. Failure doesn't scare me as much as remaining stagnant, paralyzed with fear thus never daring to try the new things.

One day, surfing the internet, I happened upon a phrase which I now consider the 'theme' of how I live my life: *Irrational Optimism*. Yes! That is so me. The concept resonated to my very soul. Irrational Optimism. I so strongly believe, against all odds, that what I do will work, the fear part of the equation is almost negligible. Oh, I admit I might still wake up in the middle of the night anxiously questioning, 'Why am I doing this? Oh no! What have I done?' But I know it's always the darkest before the dawn and, come morning, my fear will be gone. It wasn't ever easy but I have learned to trust and have faith in myself.

I could have travelled down many different paths but I choose to be who and what I am today. I have never really been motivated by money, probably due to the lack of it growing up, however I do realize how much it allows me to help others, and, through helping others, to help myself. Now, at this stage of my career, philanthropy is quickly becoming my life's work. Money has always been drawn to me and I believe when you take the focus off the money and do what you love, life just brings you everything you need.

I really relish being a leader, guiding others based on my experiences so they too can learn, as I have, from my mistakes and, of course, from my life's triumphs as well. Irrational Optimism, that's what it takes. I want to promote that concept because it's just what the world needs today. Yes, that and the other lessons so essential to professional and personal success. Stand up for justice. Forgive the forgivable, but don't condone any B.S. Work hard for what you want, but never lie because it'll come back and bite you in the *ASS*umption and never, never, ever give up on what you love.

Gina Best

Gina Best is a serial entrepreneur and a maverick coach who compels business owners to deal with their personal shit so they can attack their businesses with passion and authenticity. Gina owns one of BC's largest mortgage broker alliance, coaches entrepreneurs, speaks to and inspires audiences across the continent, and still finds – rather *makes* – time to be a mostly patient mom to two wild boys, a dependable friend, shoe hoarder, and mentor to young business women in her community.

Gina has it all and she earned it – through hard work, tears (like full out sobs), anger, self-doubt, grit, and hustle.

Website: www.gina.best

Chapter 8

Vulnerability Saved My Life

By Gina Best

I used to have a theoretical rule book. A thick one in my mind that I lived by. *Don't let them see you cry. Be strong. Busy is good. Feelings are for pansies.* Rules to live by. To do work by. To have relationships by. I thought they were etched in stone. The foundation of my controlling ways.

For most of my life, I've been a huge control freak. And being a control freak worked for me for a long time. (At least, I thought it did.) I fell into an opportunity and ran with it. When opportunity knocked, I answered. And I turned that nugget of an opportunity into a multi-million-dollar business. I worked hard, set my goals, and figured it out along the way.

I kept tight control over everything. A death grip, really. The result: success (on everyone else's terms as I'd learn much later). I was important. I won awards and made a name for myself in the industry. I felt significant and validated. I had proof that I was good enough. That I could be successful at something. The more awards I won, the more successful I felt I was. After all, plaques with your name engraved are symbols of success, right? I was someone important; I had the proof. The awards said so. The money said so.

But inside the truth was: I was miserable. Unhappy. Unfulfilled. Not feeling successful at all.

You see, when I started the company, there was a *big* void in my life that I was filling subconsciously. A massive chasm that I didn't want to look at anymore. So when the financial planning firm I worked for gave me the opportunity to be their mortgage broker, I said *yes*. And began to grow my 'baby.' Over the next 12 years, I grew the business from $0 to $120,000,000. I worked really hard, networked my ass off at 4 to 5 events a week, and built real relationships, which became the foundation of the business. One very one-sided relationship at a time. (It was always about them, never about me. 'Me' was stuffed down in that chasm I was so strategically filling with success, money, and plaques.) I didn't allow myself to want for anything; I was focused on work and on others only.

I was a sponge. I absorbed everything I could. I took courses, hired coaches, and talked to every expert who'd share information with me. And what I didn't know, I figured it out as I went along. I had some really successful ideas. And I had some really unsuccessful ones too. I fell on my face more times than I can count. I'd brush it off, get up, and keep going. I did this for many years. I created a world where I was important and others knew it. I became the go-to person for those around me. I shared what I learned and helped in many ways. I created a world that I had control. (The control freak in me loved it!)

So I kept going. Doing more and more. Busy was my religion; I would fill my time with work and taking care of others. When I wasn't working I made sure my time was filled so I didn't have to address the big, deep, tough questions that had been trying to creep up for over a decade: *"Is this it?!"* and *"How is this my life?"* I didn't know the answer to them and I was very afraid of addressing them. So I tucked them away—far, far away. (In my imagination, there was a door and I would visualize it shutting, hiding all the tough stuff away.) *How could this be?* I had it all. Great business, money in the bank, amazing kids, lots of friends and a huge social circle. My life was the definition of success. *Right?*

Wrong.

I had success, sure, but I was missing something. I just didn't know what it was. And the search for that missing something plagued me for a long time. In the few moments when my guard was down, the question would creep in again. I didn't like the feeling incomplete, so I would just find something else to do. Anything but acknowledge that I wasn't whole. I figured if I was too busy to pay attention to the yearning, it would go away. (It didn't. Even though I fought it tooth and nail.)

How could I not be ok with where I was? I had it *all!* The voice in my head refused to listen to my gut. And it got mean. It screamed at me: *"How dare you, Gina!? You're greedy and selfish!* For a long time, I listened to it. In fact, I believed it. So I carried on: working more, rushing home to be mom, and filling any gaps with other people and their needs. I made sure everyone was happy, supported, and taken care of. I forgot to take care of me.

Then one day, in a rare moment of bravery, I asked myself a very tough question: "Where do you fall on your own priority list?" The answer was jarring: I wasn't even on my priority list. Huge mistake.

During the safety demonstration on airplanes, they always say "Put your own oxygen mask on before you assist others." It is the same in life. We know we should come first, and yet time and time again we put ourselves last. I was really good at being last. And the cost to me was detrimental (thankfully, not irreversible). Emotionally, mentally, and physically- I was destroyed.

Let me explain.

In 1997, just after my husband and I got married, we decided to start a family. It was soooo much fun practicing yet it wasn't working. When it didn't happen naturally, we went to a fertility clinic for help. We got lucky: pregnant with twins! When I told my husband, he was so excited. He's the kind of guy who wanted a football team of his own. He was elated, but for me it was different. I had a bad feeling deep down.

At 9 weeks, I felt a sharp pain as I was leaving work. Blood followed. An ultrasound showed that I was still pregnant, but now with only one.

Another 9 weeks later on a Friday, I felt off. Not unusual for a woman who's 4 ½ months pregnant. But it was different. I knew something bad was happening. And I was terrified. In fact, I was too scared to even move—in case I dislodged the baby. The weekend was quiet and still. On Monday, in a haze of pain, my son was born in the bathroom. My dream of becoming a mom slipped away. He would never take a breath.

For a month afterward, I avoided everyone and everything. I'd stay up all night and sleep all day. In December, I diverted my pain to crafts and made hundreds of clove oranges (trust me, no one needs—or can give away—hundreds of clove oranges). Every time I pushed a clove into an orange, I pricked my thumb and I felt the pain. This was the only pain I would allow. I refused to talk about the babies. I refused to grieve.

By January, I was back at work. And all of the feelings of grief, loss, anger, sadness were locked away in the vault. I resumed 'normal' activities (whatever normal is). That's when I started my first company, 'the baby' that I grew. It was mine, and I had full control, which was important. With that control I could keep the emotions locked away. I could do things my way. I could manipulate those around me. I could lie and say 'I'm an open book' and tell everyone what they wanted to hear yet never ever let anyone close enough to learn about me.

A decade later, I was plagued by the idea that something was missing. So, like as usual, I decided to ignore it and become even busier. So I started another company. I thought if I took this on I could fill my void with doing. More time in the office meant less time dealing with my shit. I jumped in, took a leap of faith, got the license, hired a great partner, and then... I freaked out. *How was I going to do this!? What the hell am I doing!?*

My freak out led me to Dov Baron's Authentic Speaker Academy for Leadership. A friend of mine had taken the program and the changes in him were amazing. Prior to the Academy, he was one of those guys with 'crazy' energy around him – not the good kind. He suggested (strongly) that I join the program. In fact, he hounded me. I signed up just to get him to stop.

The day I spoke to Dov for the first time I knew something huge was going to happen. I had no idea what I was getting myself into but I knew I had to do it. I put my head between my knees and signed on the dotted line, committing to the program and, unbeknownst to me at the time, to dealing with my shit.

A few months later, I found myself in a roomful of strangers thinking *what the hell am I doing here?* I knew I wanted (and really needed) something different and that this was the starting point, but still it took everything I had in me not to bolt from that room. I stayed. And that day *'courage to change my life'* became my mantra. It stays with me to this day.

That weekend was the starting point for the rest of my life. That weekend challenged everything I thought I knew about myself. It changed everything.

On Day 3, at 6:01 pm, Dov stood before us and asked "what is your biggest shame?" My first reaction: "I don't have shame." After all, I was fine. Totally *fine!* I didn't do shame. I spent years avoiding that shameful pit in my stomach. Then a tiny little voice whispered to me: "Gina: the babies." That was my shame.

My head screamed *no!* But my heart took over and I got up, took the microphone, and for 16 minutes, I spoke about something I had no idea I had attached such shame to. It was in that moment that the wall I had spent 15 years building crumbled.

The secret I had carried alone for all those years was exposed. The shame I felt in not being able to bear healthy children was out for all to see. The shame of not being good enough—the whole room saw it. I was a fraud. The biggest shocker? I had no idea that I had been keeping this secret. It was buried so deep I had no idea it was there. Yet once I let it out, the relief I felt was unbelievable. I felt literal weight lift from my shoulders. I was free.

The weeks that followed were a blur. Letting my secret out meant that it *all* came out. I was an opened faucet. The grief that I had held inside so tightly for years was right in front of my face and it began to seriously kick my ass. At first, I fought it. My mentor looked me in the eye: "Gina, you have to go there." With conviction, I said: "I don't want to go there." But, once you learn something about yourself, once you set your secrets free, there is no going back to that locked place.

So I went there.

I revisited the past—reluctantly. I kicked and screamed my way through it. It wasn't pretty and it wasn't easy. It came to a head when I was on a trip without my family and the grief swallowed me whole. I just simply could not fight it anymore. It hit me like a freight train. It took me to my knees – literally in the shower at Club Med in Cancun, Mexico. I sobbed for the babies I never got to hold.

It was my lowest moment. And it was the moment that helped me rise. It was the beginning of a huge change for me. In that moment, I had clarity: just because this is what I built, doesn't mean this is the way it has to be. *F**k the rules*! I made them and I can change them. I gave myself permission to want something different and to stop doing life the way I had been. I decided that it was time to listen to my heart. To go after what my soul was craving.

The first step for me was to face the heartbreak and the grief. No more hiding. Being busy had been my coping mechanism. I had been bulldozing my way through life to avoid my feelings. My stealth ability to avoid vulnerability at all costs earned me some joking from my course mates: "Gina doesn't even know how to spell the word vulnerable!" I hid behind my boldness, bright hair, and big social circles. I used my tongue as a sword to keep others at arm's length. I used my calendar as the ultimate excuse not to connect with others. My grip on control was amazing. The rules that I lived by were crazy and they were rules I'd manufactured to chain me down.

As my journey toward vulnerability unraveled, a few things became clear. Most importantly, I had uncovered the missing piece. The void. It was me. I was missing was me. And by paying attention to me first, success took on a new glow. My mortgage business has grown. My relationships became richer—and reciprocal. Now that I am truly present with others, more people come to me and I let them in to see the real me. I have more and more referrals coming to me. In 2015 I worked 80% less time and made 35% more money. 2016 has been even better.

Fifteen years ago, I took an opportunity and turned it into a huge success by being busy. It used to be my everything. Now, it's just a piece of a multi-layered me. That second company I started with an open heart *is* my heart. I speak and coach. I share my learnings with others on stage or one on one. Together we build a plan of action and identify what is hiding below the surface. It's immensely rewarding. This is where I am content. This is where I need to be for me, for my heart, and for others. I am following my heart and doing what I was meant to do. There are naysayers, sure. And it's hard work, yes. And it would definitely be easier to just continue in the mortgage world. But the easy road is overrated.

The moral of this story:

You first. You are priority number one. You are the most important person in your life. The most important person in your business. You are the heart and soul of your life. You can settle for success as others define it *or* you can strive for real success. The kind that feels right and doesn't leave nagging questions.

If you don't like where you are, change direction. If you're struggling, talk about it. If you're feeling lost, look inside you. You are the author of your story. You choose what success looks like for you.

The lessons I've learned along the way have served me well in life and business. They were hard earned. The years I spent burying my emotions hurt me and took a toll on me. Five months ago, I was diagnosed with breast cancer. And it wasn't surprising. After all those years of control, denial, and busy, the hurt manifested itself in illness.

This is your life. Now is the time. Deal with your shit.

Clear it. And grab success on your own terms.

Grace Lanni

Grace Lanni is an award-winning entrepreneur, author, speaker and certified personal branding strategist of The Branding Glass™ – a complete system to understand, design, and launch your personal brand. RSE Consulting, Grace's first business launched in '99, continues to drive sales, marketing and operational success for clients. The Managing Director of eWomen Network – Austin, Grace inspires a community of women business leaders to grow personally and professionally.

Delighted by her client's personal and career stories, Grace empowers business leaders, entrepreneurs and executives to take an active role (online & offline) to nurture their personal brand focused on ideal audiences.

www.TheBrandingGlass.com

www.facebook.com/The-Branding-Glass

@thebrandingglass

Chapter 9

Keeping it Weird

By Grace Lanni

Austin is known for many things: art in many forms, boutique wine/beer making, a top 5 'Best city to live in America,' and the '91 slogan: 'Live music capital of the world.' Austin's 'Keep it weird' slogan launched in 2000 was focused on eclectic small business growth. Austin managed to maintain its '99 small town feel in the face of continually outpacing other large US cities in growth by design.

Sipping a latte at a downtown cafe, I was again surprised at the physical changes in our city since I arrived 20 years ago. Austin embraced me as a first-time entrepreneur, and my failures were buffered by my city's passionate desire for me to succeed.

I awaited Julie, a first-time entrepreneur who had a good idea. Not yet launched, she was struggling with how to launch, make money and carve out time for her family. I saw this decision scenario repeatedly, and each person has a different appetite for entrepreneurship and a unique success profile.

I caught a flurry out of the corner of my eye. She's wasn't late, but rushed to be on time. I encouraged her to get herself a drink, and watched her interact with the people in line and behind the counter. Julie was present to those around her meeting them with a smile and a kind word. *Good,* I said to myself, a leader needs to be aware of the world around them.

Steaming coffee in hand, Julie broke out her notebook, looked me in the eye, and said that she was grateful for my interest in her consumer healthcare idea. She was anxious about all the different ideas in her head, and the reality was, she didn't know what to do next. I smiled, pleased that Julie was willing to ask for help. This is an easy item for some, and near impossible for others. Whether she accepted the help is another matter. We would see.

We'd met on and off for several months spending our time on more tactical questions, like, "Can you recommend a good startup CFO?" I decided to take a step back and ask a few general questions. I started with: "Why do you want to bring this idea to life?"

Julie's answer was filled with domain knowledge - she had a master's level education and many years in her field. She and her wellness clients were frustrated with repeating the same health background info, and whether conscious or not, they often left out details between one provider and the next. Julie wanted to provide a software solution for a consumer to collaborate with their providers. I was keen on the idea and had quite a bit of domain expertise myself.

I was less interested in the knowledge and skills she carried throughout her corporate career than the passion she expressed behind her story. As a first-time entrepreneur, she had to not only have the will, but the staying power to drive the solution and the ability to tell a compelling story. Julie had to choose between self-funding and securing outside funds – whether an angel, bank, grant or crowd funding – to succeed, her passion had to be evident to her funding audience and prospective clients.

My first Angel & Venture funded project was a software company. My passion for delivering our solution was fueled by my team, my investors, and mostly by my prospective clients who were clamoring for our finished product. We were solving a major pain for them. Prior to receiving venture funding, my team and I spent 11 months working for free. It was extremely stressful as a single Mom, not only being away from my young children, but also watching my savings & 401k deplete and credit card debt mount. I was looking for Julie's fierce devotion to her project to surmount her first revenue success mountain.

I presented my next question: "What does entrepreneurship mean to you?"

Julie sat back and thought. I could tell that she'd spent enough time with me to know that I wasn't looking for a canned, off-the-cuff answer. Julie sipped her coffee and shared from her heart. This was her first entrepreneurial venture. For her, entrepreneurship meant betting on herself and her ability to prequalify customer interest in the product and securing enough revenue for her, her team, and to grow the business. She knew enough to surround herself with mentors who would guide her in the right direction. Julie shared that she had to put her oxygen mask on first – exercise, eat right, and be in constant communication with her husband and kids about what she's doing and how grateful she is for their support. She shared that "Entrepreneurship is like sky diving for the first time, I suspect. You study, prepare, get instructors, and at some point, you jump."

I couldn't help but smirk a bit. The 'mask' comment I mentioned to her during our first meeting. During my first run to revenue, I ran myself into the ground and was out for a week. 30-something, eager, no idea what entrepreneurship meant to me or others. Julie's reference to her team and 'our company' and 'our product' was also a great pointer to the responsibility she's taking. Regardless if you're launching a solo-coaching company or a company with employees, your efforts will touch many other people around you. Are you taking your efforts seriously? Your health seriously?

As entrepreneurs, we are regularly faced with the question to keep going with our venture or to take a j-o-b or just to quit. At month 10, (just prior to being awarded $MM from a venture firm), I begged a colleague to get me an entry-level job at his powerhouse company. Thankfully, I persevered.

I believe Julie's running up against another decision point. How will she get her software developed? Dollars, convertible debt, stock, investments are all considerations. She must find what works for her.

Over the last few months, Julie has been discussing her in-house and advisory team strategies with me. Those willing to help her launch a business are a key tangible value point she can leverage to secure new prospects, great vendors (i.e. development partners or staff), and more. The wrong team member or bad advice can cost precious dollars and time, and maybe even key team members.

How do you protect your company? Trust and verify. Get references, watch what people are doing, allow your team to contribute and celebrate your milestones. There is a gut feeling about a team member that an entrepreneur must develop which could fly in the face of the seemingly great advice coming from others.

Being successful in business requires that you become solid at choosing who to work with and that you stay alert, regularly assess the value of those you work with, and promote or retire as needed. Hone your communication skills regularly! The better you become sharing your vision, giving direction, listening to grievances, negotiating, and knowing if, and when to speak at all, the better you are able to guide your business to success.

One example of a teaming issue for me came years later when I slowly forged a partnership for my consulting business. I enjoyed working with this partner, and we quickly did a few small projects together. Next, we pursued a national account and took on a larger project. Over time, this partner started to confide in me the challenges with money and staff they were having. All was not well behind their curtain. My radar was up. They pushed me to pay them within 24 hours of receiving client funds so they could pay their rent. Soon after, their investor partner wanted to meet. The investor wanted me to be an executive in their business – curious being that he didn't know a thing about our operating budget or procedures. I suspected they wanted me to simply sell projects for them. Being cautious, I stalled deeper partnership activities to see how our current project played out. I also began looking for other partners to deliver the mobile app development work my clients needed. The national project did not go well, and I lost what could have been a great client relationship. I retired that partnership immediately following this project deliverable.

Initially, I did not have enough information to avoid this failure. My rule of thumb in partnership is to go slow, pay attention, and communicate. I missed the personal connection I had with that team, but our personal connection did not delay my decision to sever future work activities. Thank goodness, our solid brand reputation allowed my firm to move forward without major issues.

Some people have a great knack for balancing the data points and their gut feel leading up to a decision. Some are terrified to make a decision without consensus from their entire team. I can tell you, that is exhausting for all concerned. An entrepreneurial leader will weigh the data, check their gut, and decide. The process doesn't end there – a leader will continually monitor the path they've set to ensure progress is being made. If not, it is likely an original assumption was faulty or something changed (which by the way, happens a lot). Entrepreneurship is not for the faint of heart! One of the most challenging things to do is let go of a team member. Only you can determine what works for you.

Julie had weathered a change on her internal team as well as one of her advisors over the last 9 months. I asked her to describe the challenge she was having with her CFO.

She shared that her CFO seemed so interested in what they were doing. He had a track record of successfully being a CFO through Angel and VC funding rounds with several other software startups. His references checked out. He seemed to have an appetite to work for free while they raised their funding. Ultimately, Julie couldn't get him on the phone to prepare for investor meetings.

At my suggestion, Julie started interviewing other early stage CFOs. A new CFO candidate, Rob, returned her calls, did his homework, and not only made himself available to prepare for an investor meeting, but also introduced Julie to a few new investors.

The most difficult part was speaking with her prior CFO. Being authentic and transparent is a key part of her brand and this project. She shared that she was open and honest and it allowed them to part ways amicably. It was not without heartache on her part.

I praised Julie for her willingness to serve the company and its future. Julie is on her way toward building a solid team that resonates with her personal brand. During our very first meeting, I asked Julie: "What is your personal brand and how does this project compliment you?"

Today, months into her first venture, Julie confessed she was most interested in my ability to start and fund businesses. She knew my current speaker platform was personal branding, but she didn't think personal branding had anything to do with launching a business.

Julie began to describe how everything she does generates her personal brand. People join her team, advise and invest based on her ability to communicate her brand authentically. A key part of her leadership activity is speaking and posting/commenting about consumer healthcare solutions. She continues to express her gratitude for her marketing team and how they help to keep her up to date on what's happening in their market. Julie's beginning to be known as the 'consumer healthcare entrepreneur.' She receives random calls from magazines and other networking contacts who were referred to me through social channels.

When we surveyed Julie's network for my personal branding attributes, I could see people thought she was corporate square by the way she dressed and spoke.

That day, Julie's outfit was professional and approachable. Austin, hip. The biggest change in Julie was her confidence. The way she held herself, interacted with people behind the counter, and even how she engaged me showed me that she was growing up as an entrepreneur. I've watched her social posts and especially like she is expressing her point of view. Julie's personal brand is driving the value of her software project, as well. The more people know Julie as the go-to person in her market, the more credible she is as a CEO. Julie is no longer the shy corporate refugee, but an entrepreneur!

We jumped into discussing other areas of her company brand – her website, specifically. Julie shared that once we worked through her personal brand profile, she gave it and a description of her software to a designer. The designer shared that her materials made it easy to develop concepts for their logo, and now she is finalizing her first website. The personal brand informed the content and visual pieces – it all fits together! Next week, she films her intro video just in time for a meeting with a key strategic partner.

Julie shared that she never expected to be handling all these projects in addition to developing a software solution. She had an idea to serve her customers, but limited clarity on exactly how they would solve the many glaring customer problems or how many moving parts would be needed to form, fund and grow a business. She's clear the business has a momentum of its own now.

Many of my clients who leave the corporate world to launch their own businesses go through the same stages. Simon is moving from Europe and planning to launch a new firm here in Austin. He is starting from scratch with his brand, social media, website, team, partners, etc. He's already established himself as a specialized development resource in his country, but retained our firm to support his transition. It can be scary to make the jump from corporate to entrepreneur. Imagine making the move to a new country at the same time!

Next, I asked Julie: "What does your support system look like these days?"

Like many first-time CEOs, Julie thought she was her only support system. Then, Kristi joined her team and helped with the marketing aspects – doing research, calling prospective clients and partners, etc. Next, Kristi brought on another person part-time to help with social media. Now she also has a CFO, CIO, attorney, and advisory team. Julie's not fully operational yet, but feels like she's ready for her first investment to develop her first application and their beta sales pipeline.

Julie didn't forget to mention her family as part of her support system, either. Her husband and kids are so much a part of her life; she took my advice and created a weekly update dinner for her family. This dinner conversation keeps them insulated from the monstrous ups and downs in the business day to day activity and shows them how much she appreciates the freedom to launch her project. They are behind Julie 100%, and she's able to ask them what activities are most important to them in the upcoming week and to schedule most of her meetings around their needs.

Wow, I was struck by this response from Julie. She was repeating back to me how she applied my first founder story and the importance of acknowledging family. I smiled inside as I recognized that she had successfully applied her transparency personal branding attribute at home. She is aligning her personal and business lives to reflect her values.

Personal/business brand alignment makes it easier to nurture your 'gut reaction' to any challenge. When you operate from your authentic self, it is more natural to make decisions which align with your values.

Today, I'm in the middle of launching a new personal branding platform into a broader market. I am grateful to be part of the eWomen Network global organization which provides vehicles to promote my content, my books, training and a success system to support my next level of growth.

The last question for Julie today was: "Where do you see yourself in 5 years?"

Julie commented that her mind was racing from the questions we discussed. She gets trapped in the minutia of the next step, and forgets to take time to painting her vision.

In 5 years, Julie sees herself as an advisor to this company. She's successfully funded, launched, and sold her collaborate healthcare software solution – all while maintaining self-care and acknowledging her family. She's worked very hard for 5 years, and a large national firm acquired her business. She envisions in 5 years working about 20 hours per week focused on strategy and positioning the solution with key strategic partners globally. She makes lunches for her kids, picks them up from school, and travels as a family around the world furthering her healthcare collaboration vision. New ideas for features pop up, and she's able to feed those to the product marketing team for vetting and development without getting buried in the doingness.

There will be hurdles and pivots along the way for Julie. Sometimes, you, dear reader, will seem like the universe is lining up the world to fulfil your next vision. It is your personal vision. Update it, post it on your bathroom mirror, in your office, use it to calm you when things get wonky – because it will. Though there are times to be tactical and focus on operational details and your 100-day plan. Don't forget to pick your head up and review the landscape of your business. I suspect you'll know exactly where to start from there.

What's my answer to the truth about success in business? Know your authentic values, express them consistently in the world, review your vision often and enjoy the ride.

Buono Viajare, Grace Lanni.

Heather Andrews

Heather is a certified health coach with 26 years of experience in healthcare coupled with a passion for helping women find health, harmony and happiness. In her coaching business she helps women take control of their lives using the art and science of habit change which takes a 360-degree approach unique to your life and motivating factor to introduce your real life to your ideal life.

Heather has a full-time career and an online business and is raising 3 teenagers! When her husband was deployed to Afghanistan, she created the secret formula to raising children as a solo parent and running a successful business.

With her experience and certifications as a healthcare professional, manager, change mentor, and health coach, she is the founder of Follow it Thru Health Coaching and creator of the MOM on the Go program.

www.followitthru.com

www.facebook.com/groups/empoweredmoms123

Chapter 10

5 Simple Steps for Sustaining a Successful Business and Life

By Heather Andrews

I have experienced moments in my life that have brought me to my knees. These were truly pivotal moments! I not only survived, but flourished. I found how I reacted in those moments determined the direction my life took, who I have become and the growth I experienced was astounding for the foundation I set for my life and my business.

Our stories and experiences drive us forward and we overcome from what we learn. It is about the journey and not the destination.

One of the powerful life altering moments was a phone call from my husband telling me that he was being recalled to active US Military duty in Afghanistan for 18 months! After 10 years of him being a reservist, I never dreamed this would happen. I felt throat punched and wondered how I would tell our three children that their dad was going to a country where they knew people died.

He was headed to the frontlines and I felt the same for me as I was upfront and alone with our children.

How would I survive with three kids, a full-time career, and a successful business? I had no choice. Others moms did this, right? It would just mean I'd be busy.

The day came for him to leave and I felt sick inside. While I knew it wasn't going to be forever, the idea of solo parenting three children under eight felt so overwhelming that I went back to bed and cried.

Two months in, I was emotionally and physically burnt out from my daily routine of working, running a side business, raising my kids and running them to all their activities. I was done. I knew something had to change. My life was spinning out of control.

I wondered what people would think of me if I admitted I couldn't do it all. I am not a superhero! The realization that I could probably not and did not want to do this made me reclaim my time and sanity so I could find a solution that worked for us as a family. Everyday our calendar was jam packed with sports, school events and other activities and I felt like I had the weight of the world on my shoulders. My business was also taking a hit as I could not properly serve all my clients.

Regardless of what other people thought, the chaos had to stop. If you're struggling with your businesses, I'm sure you'll understand the pressure I felt to keep my head above water.

In order to survive, I had Plan A and Plan B which included these 5 key steps which today, have become the foundation for my Mom on the Go Program:

1. Master Your Time.

   Everyone complains about never having enough time to do all the things they need to do. But have you ever taken a good hard look at exactly *where* you are spending your time? Chances are, you're caught up doing things that are better off left undone, delegated to someone else or can be done at a different time.

   To start, track how long you are on social media. That one is always a shocker and a parasitic time sucker!

   I put everything into one calendar to begin to get a grip on how full my schedule was-a picture is worth 1000 words.

2. Set Healthy Boundaries.

   Do you feel wracked with guilt if you say no to someone? Do you feel judged for saying no? What I have learned is that as soon as you respect yourself (and your time) enough to say no, and give yourself permission to do so, your world will change.

   We live by our choices. It's about focus and priorities. Modern life, especially for mothers does have the potential to become unmanageably overwhelming, making us feel hopeless and tired, which makes everything in life seem much worse.

   When I decided to start taking care of my own needs, as well as my family's, things changed.

   Setting boundaries is about self-survival and good self-care hygiene is not selfish. The best give you can give yourself is learning to say *no!*

3. Communicate Your Needs

    Even though my kids were only eight, five and three, I sat them down and explained, "Daddy will be gone for another 16 months, doing his work so we need to work together to make things easier for all of us."

    My oldest two children and I talked through our weekly schedule. Surprisingly, there were activities that could be easily eliminated because they didn't like going to them anyway! Who knew?

4. Manage Your Stress

    Stressors are everywhere! If you look in the mirror and say you're not good enough, like I did, known as self-inducing stress, how the heck do you think others are going to look at you differently? If you're running ragged and feel like you're out of control, you probably are. If you feel overwhelmed, take a moment to realize that your decisions and actions created this situation.

    Stress is becoming the number one health epidemic according to the World Health Organization. It affects weight, sleep and overall health. Luckily, we had the capacity to think and choose differently from this point forward. Once I figured that out, I knew I was on the way to becoming the boss of my own world and you can too.

5. Ask for Help

    If the car is running on empty, you won't reach your destination!

    As a depleted, burnt-out business owner/mom, what are the chances that you can give your children or clients what they need? Once you admit that you need help, and respect yourself enough to ask for it, your world will change.

Little did I realize that by doing these five things I not only changed the course of my life, but also that of my kids and my business.

Take a moment and ask yourself these 3 questions:

1. Is it possible I'm not as efficient with my time as I possibly can be? Do I work every second and never have any downtime?

2. Do I refuse to delegate things because it's easier to do it myself?

3. Am I doing things that serve my family or do I just like to look like I'm super busy because that's what others do?

If you answer yes to any of these questions, you really need to get control of your time before you burn out like I did.

As business women and moms, we have a lot stacked against us.

I'm living proof that this stuff works!

Our Results:

We mastered our time by eliminating the activities the kids did not like. I realized that my time was my most important commodity and took care of how I spent it. Today if something does not give me joy, allow me to feel fulfilled or doesn't allow me to add to my bottom line then it does not get added to my calendar. I am busy but it's scheduled. The way I spend my time serves my vision and passion for my life. Once I made this change, my life and that of my family changed for the better.

I set my boundaries and learned to say no and realized I wasn't going to be everything to everyone. I also made sure to include downtime in my calendar. I realized that this was not selfish but self-survival and good self-care. My guilt decreased and I was happier and had more energy to be the best me! Before taking anything on, I now ask myself, "Why am I doing this?" I'm also mindful of the 'invisible boundary' that entrepreneurs often encounter when attempting to step out of their comfort zones. Fear of the unknown can hold you back from going after your goals. So be aware of your boundaries and what their purpose is.

I started communicating my needs to my children. They were old enough to help with small tasks and it eliminated the overwhelm, stress and disorganization and made them feel good about contributing. This has carried forward to today. Communication is key when asking for help from your business team, your support and your cheerleaders. Just because you are building a business and spend hours on your laptop, does not mean the world stops around you. If you forget about the relationships of those around you, your journey to the top will be a lonely one. As you grow and expand, communication is key to your success for you and your team so you may as well start early and set the habit and foundation.

After implementing these three key tools, my stress was drastically reduced and I could look in the mirror and say *good job!* I felt empowered and this reaffirmed my self-worth, I no longer cared about what others thought because I was proud of what I created for my family and my business.

I always told my kids, it didn't matter what happened during the day, as long as they could look at themselves in the mirror at night and say they did their best that day. The same goes for your business. If you're proud of what you are creating, it puts a fire in your belly, and you take empowered action each and every day, then your business will thrive. Take the control out of the out of control and your life will run like a well-oiled machine.

Asking for help may not always mean your family. It has to be the right help. As your business grows, your needs change and you may need a mentor, a coach, or someone to lean on and keep you accountable and your mindset in check. I ask my family for help daily as I can't do everything on my own, nor was I meant to. We are not meant to do life alone. I hired a business coach and mindset coach. It was an investment in me and part of my self-care. And it's allowed me to be the best for myself, my family and my clients.

Taking care of yourself also means having fun, celebrating your wins, and taking a break along the way. I recently forgot about this and as soon as I took a break, my creativity and appreciation came flowing back.

Remember, it's ok to ask for help! You're not perfect and that is ok. Being flawed and perfectly imperfect is more fun and laughter is good for the soul!

These techniques and habits are the foundation for success in life *and* business and still exist in our house today. And I am proud to say that my young adult children have adopted them as well.

All of the lessons I learned, from these pivotal moments in my life, led to the creation of my business, Follow it Thru. My passion project, Mom On the Go was created so that you, as mothers, entrepreneurs, and business women don't have to go through what I did.

Has this journey been easy? Heck no! But it was absolutely worth it! What has made it easier is that I have the tools, habits, and a strong foundation to keep moving forward. I still have to set boundaries and break through them. I have had stressful days but also a hell of a lot of fun building new relationships and celebrating my wins. I have cried when things did not go well and I have cried with clients at their breakthroughs. I realized along the way, that in order to help people transform, I had to transform and oh boy, what a journey it has been.

I have discovered more about myself in the last two years. I have run successful businesses in the past in my twenties, thirties, and forties. It is a skill on its own. You are selling yourself to the world and it takes creativity, bravery, and vision. The biggest thing I learned was if one piece of your life is out of alignment, chances are everything is. When you embark on a business, it takes consistent action each day and things don't always go well. You must be able to react and have the resilience to move on.

With each business I have operated, I have learned habits and knowledge to set the foundation for success. The foundation must be strong to build a successful business. Each step on my journey through entrepreneurship has felt like a Lego brick building on another. I am still building my masterpiece and that's the best part of the journey.

Every step forward, every person you meet, is an opportunity. Trust your intuition and be open to receiving these opportunities. This isn't always easy but it's so worth it! At the end of the day, I want to live my life for ninety years versus living the same year ninety times. We only have one life and don't you deserve to live the life you truly *deserve?*

You have chosen this book for a reason. Each co-author has overcome challenge and adversity. We are building our dreams and legacy; something bigger than ourselves. Embrace what we have shared with you.

No business started big. Small beginnings lead to big results. Think about *your* pivotal moments and how you can use them to change the world and fulfill your soul. I want you to find the same fulfillment and passion in your life as I have in mine.

At the end of the day, I am the boss of my own world and the discoveries and the feeling of putting your shoulders back and being proud of what you have built, there is no other feeling like it.

Imagine what that would feel like for you!

Janet Wiszowaty

Janet's adventurous spirit is seen in everything she does, from a 30-year career with the Royal Canadian Mounted Police as an emergency dispatcher to creating programs to help First Responders and those who have suffered a trauma to move forward. She created FamilyConnekt to bring people and resources together and hosts an internet radio show to share knowledge to those who are unable to travel to learn from her guests. Janet's motto is "Life is a team sport and when we all work together miracles happen."

www.familyconnekt.com

Worldly Connektions on tlrstation.com

www.facebook.com/janet.wiszowaty

Chapter 11

The Hills and Valleys
of Business and Life

By Janet Wiszowaty

I think many people dream of having a business. My first memory of wanting to make money was making mats out of newspapers and thinking I could sell them and make money. I had found the pattern to do this in a book when I was about 10 years old. I would find newspapers and weave them into mats, I had lots of mats but no sales. I started babysitting when I was 11 and when I was 13 I got a paper route and managed to get enough new subscribers to win a trip to Winnipeg, pretty exciting for a 13 year old who lived in a town of 500 people. My drive to make some money was to be able to purchase a horse for myself. I didn't buy the horse, one was given to me and I bought myself a saddle, bridle and paid for my horses feed and board

As the years went on and my teachers reinforced the idea that I wasn't very smart those ideas slowly faded from my vision. My parents worked hard to give us things they never had and growing up in the 50's and 60's my future was to get married and have a family. According to many, I was not smart enough to go to university and other careers considered to be good ones for women at that time were of no interest to me. I ended up getting a job as a bank teller, married at 18 and 2 children by 22. As I was raising my children I worked part time in a bank and did the wife and mommy thing.

In 1981, I literally fell into my job with the Royal Canadian Mounted Police. I was asked if I would be interested in filling in for maternity leave and as I was married to an R.C.M.P. member it was easier for them to do a security clearance on me on short notice. As it turned out, I loved the job and ended up joining as a Civilian Member in 1982 as an emergency police dispatcher. That job changed my life! Not in the way you may think but because I met Liz Mannix. Liz had a Master's Degree in Education and told me I was smart enough to go to university and encouraged me to write the mature student entry exam. I passed it and was accepted, since then I have been accepted into 6 universities/ colleges. My husband's career took us to different provinces and cities and with each move I continued my studies wherever we went.

As my career with the R.C.M.P. continued and I accumulated more and more university credits I thought my life was pretty good. Until a very dark night in January 2003. My husband and I had been in a very bad car accident the previous August and I was off work due to my physical and mental injuries. 5 months after the accident I was sitting alone in my dark living room, everyone in the house was asleep and here I was crying and wishing I had died in that car accident. I knew at that moment I needed help. I attributed it to the multiple car accidents I had been in, 4 in 10 years.

Blessings come in the strangest ways, although at the time of the accident, I had an undiagnosed arterial venous malformation (like an aneurysm) behind my right ear, ovarian cysts that were growing and post-traumatic stress disorder from some of the calls I had taken as a police dispatcher. These were all discovered during my recovery treatments. The psychologist I saw soon revealed to me that I was not suffering from trauma due to the motor vehicle accidents but to accumulative PTSD due to my job. Thus the journey began.

We are all on a journey and sometimes it is best that we do not know all the hills and valleys we must go through to get to our destination because we may give up before we begin.

My journey into the business world began after I started training with Jack Canfield, the Chicken Soup for The Soul co-author and the author of The Success Principles. You see, I needed to keep moving forward after my time with the psychologist and my way of doing that was to take a series of self-development courses/workshops. My journey with Jack started in April 2010 when I attended a one-day event in Seattle. By the end of a seven-day training in August and a five-day training in October 2010 I was ready to begin a business. My business was to help people like myself who were ready to move forward from a crisis. I shared my idea with my two granddaughters and they came up with my business name: FamilyConnekt. I was so excited I told a man I had been referred to about branding and he advised me to get it trademarked right away...my lesson - when starting out do a little more research, ask a few more questions. This cost me up around the $5,000.00 mark to trademark my business name and then was informed it was only trademarked in the United States. Tip #1: ask lots of questions!

I have been working on/in my business since 2011. I studied Greek Mythology in university and I compare growing my business to the punishment given to Sisyphus who was condemned in the underworld (Tartarus/Hades) to push a boulder up the hill. As he reached the top of the hill, the boulder would roll down again and he had to push it back again. I do not have a business background, I trained as an emergency police dispatcher and could handle any emergency at a moment's notice. That isn't how business works and I did not have a circle of friends nor acquaintances that were in business who could help me with this new venture. I studied and went to more workshops and gained more tools to help those who were like me, struggling to keep moving forward and find meaning in a life that at times was not so bright. The one thing I didn't do was take business courses. You see, I have no interest in that, just to be of service but, being of service and helping people does not pay the bills unless you have a limitless bankroll. Tip #2: work on yourself always!

I took early retirement in 2011 so that I could continue my training with Jack Canfield and started to also do some training with Marcia Wieder (Dream Coaching). I wrote a chapter in a book and became a published author. I created workshops around the success principles I had learned from Jack Canfield and learned how to coach people to discover and go after their dreams. #Tip 3: go after your dreams.

Now I was again back to the Greek Mythology. Now I was Atlas holding up the world, helping everyone that came my way and always being the first person to volunteer and be of service. That doesn't pay the bills either, because the people I was there for did not have the means to pay me and I wanted to help them. So what if they couldn't afford it, I would help them free of charge. I would put on workshops and if they could not pay the cost of the workshop I would discount it or invite them to come as my guest.

Thus, the expenses I put out for those workshops came out of our pocket. But, I was helping people. Or, was I? Tip #4: give generously but set clear boundaries on how much you give away.

I could see so many people hurting and I was there for them yet I never seemed to be able to reach the people I considered my ideal niche, the First Responders. My big why was to be able to help those who were hurting so bad that they wanted to or did commit suicide. A young police officer I worked with shot himself 6 months after a murder suicide of a two-year-old by his father… the details of which the officer told me he could not rationalize in his head. Where was the help for him? I wanted to be that person, to be there for the next one who was going though such pain but I couldn't seem to reach them.

I listened to audios about finding your niche and once you were focused everything would fall into place. My niche was different and if anyone thinks First Responders will fall into, what I would call a normal niche, they sadly misunderstand the thinking of those heroic people. They are strong for others, are there for each other during a crisis in the line of duty. They have never been equipped to handle the stresses of their job and certainly will not admit that they have something that might even look like a mental illness - post traumatic stress disorder. Have a drink, work more overtime it will all go away and be forgotten.

It doesn't go away, I found that out when God immobilized me and made me sit in my shit! That is the night the mask cracked. All that I had kept pushed down for so long that allowed me to do my job without falling apart as I took the call from a little girl about 7 who called in at 3 am asking for us to come and help her mother who was being beat up by a boyfriend. I had a granddaughter the same age who might even be in the same class as the little girl I was speaking to. I was helpless except to send the police. If I let my feelings out I would not have been able to do my job and then I would not have been able to get help for that little girl. That's what our First Responders do, push all those feelings down so they can do their job. Tip #5: share your feelings and struggles with people who support you and love you.

For the last 5 years I have been working on/in my business. In order to keep my business going I rely heavily on my husband who keeps working full time in his second career. I contract back to the R.C.M.P. in the Eastern Arctic of Canada where I go up to the Baffin Islands and do relief dispatching so the dispatchers there can take a much needed holiday.

Why do I keep going? Well, I believe in what I do and as I keep moving forward I am meeting some amazing people who also believe in what I do. Do I always articulate what I do? No, and that comes to another area you need to know about business. Tip #6: build a team to support you.

I recently read an article by Andrea Goulet, software remodeling evangelist, CEO and Corgibytes: keynote speaker. She referenced a turning point in her role in the business her and her husband had built. Although she could code and understood the technical side of the business, she would refer to herself as non-technical. That was until the day her husband said in an interview she was non-technical and she was deeply hurt. She asked him why he would say that, his comments were "Andrea...I used the exact words you used to describe yourself at a client meeting yesterday. When you start calling yourself technical, I will too." So I ask you, what are you calling yourself? After reading this article I started thinking of what I said when I spoke to people at networking events. I rewrote my bio and started to share more about my vision for working with First Responders and those who were ready to move forward from trauma. Once I did that and embraced it everything shifted. People of influence that worked with First Responders and PTSD sufferers started to show up in my life. I was introduced to one then another and before I knew it I was where I wanted to be. I received messages from my peers on how working with me had helped them. Tip #7: shift yourself to get clear on your vision and your business will shift.

I am writing this while on a visit to Banff, Alberta in the Rocky Mountains. Today when I went for a walk I couldn't see the mountains due to the low cloud cover. As the day went on and the sun came out the majestic snow-capped mountains appeared in all their glory. If we are not finding our clients, does that mean they are not there? What if they are there just waiting for us to show up and see them. Like the snow-capped mountains I couldn't see this morning, they are just waiting for you. When I rewrote my biography and showed up everything shifted. Tip #8: your clients are right in front of you.

As you read the chapters of this book you will find there are many reasons why the other authors started their businesses and there will be stories of the ups and downs of their business. The one thing they all have in common is the desire to serve and to leave the world a better place. We have all had our tipping points that has lead us to this place of building a business. Mine was the car accident that had me immobilized long enough for me to realize I was slowly dying in the job I was doing. My health had deteriorated and in order to be well I knew something had to shift. Would I have willingly chosen all the challenges I have had along the way? No. Yet without those challenges I would not be who I am, met the people I have met or done and seen some of the things that make me who I am today. If your desire is to start a business to solely make money, that may not be a good enough reason to keep you going. Would I like more money? Yes and as each year moves on to the next, my business makes more money than the year before, which I am very grateful for. Tip #9: allow your life experiences to guide you.

I have found that although there are times I want to stay in bed all day and read a novel or be with my family every evening sitting down at dinner together, I would soon be bored. At these times there is always something that shows up to keep me going, I received the following a while ago and it is the reward behind what I do:

"I really appreciated our week together. I had quite a delay home but enjoyed some me time in the airports. Flying back by myself was not so bad, thanks for the visualization tip of my life/event taking off! My husband wondered who you were as I signed up for swimming lessons when I got home (I used to be terrified of water.) I jumped in the deep end & went down my first water slide 2 weeks ago. Thanks again for being the kind of lady that you are!"

"I had known Janet from our time working together for the R.C.M.P. and I knew what fields she worked in from our conversations there. When I was at what was probably the lowest point in my life I reached out to her. Since that time I've been on the path of getting where I want to be and her knowledge, experience and guidance have been instrumental in this. I wholeheartedly recommend speaking with Janet if you find yourself lost, with a problem and are unsure of where to go or how to proceed"

Who am I and what do I do? I am a visionary, teacher and a healer with a goal. My vision is that I see our First Responders heal from the traumas they have endured and the atrocities some of them have seen. I envision their families coming together as a unit with each member understanding how important they are to each other. I am a healer, I am dedicated to continue learning more tools, to share those tools and teach them for others to use in their own healing so they can become the masters of their own destination. My goal is that as this healing takes place and those who have lost a piece of themselves that they will find it again and become whole.

Even at times when I felt like giving up, I was compelled to keep going. I once spoke to a shaman about the feeling I was being pushed to do the work I do and she suggested I look at it as a magnet drawing me toward what I am destined to do. What are you destined to do and what are you willing to do to do it? Tip #10: keep going even when you don't feel like it.

Your business will be a success when you decide what you want your business to be. What does success mean to you? Is it to make money? If it is to make money your drive will be different than the person who is there to be of service. Can it be both? I believe it can be. Follow what makes you soul sing. There are people waiting for you to show up.

Jill Enticknap

Jill Enticknap is a rising star in the coaching, marketing and literary world. With her extensive entrepreneurial experience, supporting the growth of other businesses as well as her own brand, she has gained insight into the ups and downs of success.

She has created a 12-week program that supports her coaching clients and has witnessed clients transform in the areas of: relationships, health, business and spirituality, which she labels 'The Four Pillars of Life.'

As Jill expands her businesses and spiritual life she extends the reach of her message, which is simply: love is all there is.

http://www.jillenticknap.com/

http://www.getempowereddaily.com/

https://www.facebook.com/jill.enticknap

Chapter 12

Shut Up and Listen

By Jill Enticknap

Throughout my evolution, the statement "shut up and listen" has sparked many different reactions. In my earliest years if I heard it, I did exactly what was asked without question. As my teenage years rolled around, I absolutely rebelled against anyone and anything that wanted to influence my decisions almost doing the exact opposite in spite of the individual, or at least that was the common interpretation of my actions.

I had been raised with a completely different set of ideals then anyone I knew. This being blessing or a curse depending on which side of the coin you were on. I was raised with the belief that I was the creator of my own life, raised to be accountable for my experiences and that I could accomplish anything that I put my mind and heart to, without limitation. I was ruled by an inner compass, an inner voice, guiding me. To many, this appeared dangerous in my tiny rural Alberta town, yet to me, regardless of my consequences, it was all I knew. It led me to be independent, driven and develop a spirit ready to create success, solve problems, see multiple sides to every situation and search for the good, all being perfect ingredients for entrepreneurship. There was no problem too big, task too overwhelming, or skill that I did not believe I could cultivate if I did not already possess.

As my first business endeavour, at age 19, I ventured out and partnered in a small town restaurant in rural Alberta. This was an extremely less than ideal business decision which was pointed out by many more experienced and business savvy individuals, yet the inner compass said yes and as a result so did I. The energy, focus, perseverance and will it took to be an underfunded business startup became very clear. I quickly realized that I only saw the tip of the iceberg and there was so much more that needed to go into bringing the project to life then I could have ever imagined. I did not hesitate, I shut up and listened, dived in head first, fully committed and willing to do whatever it took to make the vision a reality. This meant stress from having to overcome lack of formal training, sleepless nights, crippled relationships, extreme learning curves, missing out on more family and friend events then I care to recall, tears…so many tears, sore feet, favours from any able body and other unforeseen challenges. This is no surprise to any experienced entrepreneur. I was tested to the max. There are always two sides to the coin. Through this experience, I was able to expand myself to extremes revealing the tip of MY true capabilities. This endeavour pushed me to lead, to be seen, to develop new skills, create new connections I still value today, it showed me who I could really count on and it was the opportunity that sparked the fire of my true entrepreneurial spirit.

Shortly after moving on from this experience, when I was 21, my mom suggested that I get into the life coaching field, thus being one of the youngest coaches in North America at the time. As much as this idea called to me, this is when I first encountered my inner demons. I could feel the rising of doubt and unworthiness within me which I am sure was always present, yet felt foreign. "Who could ever think that I had something worthwhile to say?" was what my shadow side was telling me. This lead me on a search for life experience, a search to become the person that did have something worthwhile to say, I had to develop the outer voice that matched the inner compass.

I always knew I could accomplish things I didn't know possible, and in business I was able to put this belief to the test, to expand, to fail and to get back up and try again. I honed the ability to rely on my inner compass, this leading me around the world in search of international business opportunities. I said yes to whatever came my way, that was aligned with my inner voice that would lead me to an expansion of skills and experience, allowing me to travel the world and see business in other cultures first hand. I observed different ways of life and studied different ways of doing business. I gained understanding and tolerance within myself as a result of the different cultures I encountered. I gained a deep compassion for those that had less, those who were not raised in the limitless mindset that I was and who were not born into opportunity. I developed a deep gratitude for where I had come from because of where I was lead. This was a roller coaster ride of experiences, emotions and unbelievable moments I cherish and will one-day share.

The entrepreneurial flame within me continued to burn and call with every opportunity to expand. I knew it was my time, yet next came the most profound Shut Up & Listen experience that changed it all. I attended my first 10-day, completely silent meditation retreat called Vipassana. It is a Buddhist practise that has been going on for centuries and today there are centres in over 150 countries throughout the world. It just so happened that I returned to a small camp 30 minutes from my home town to partake and develop my Shut Up and Listen practice. It is here that I dove deep within, deeper than ever before to face parts of myself I was unaware existed. It was here, in silent meditation that I experienced surrender, clarity, compassion, forgiveness, courage, unconditional love of source and self, and the discovered my true voice. I did not know it at the time but through silence I ironically unlocked my outer voice. I was finally able to align with the inner voice that had been guiding me all my life. It was here that the entrepreneurial flame engulfed me and my destiny could be denied no longer. It was in those moments of silence I saw and felt the truth.

It was time for me to do it on my own, to begin the journey of developing my own businesses, under my own model, with my own voice, grounding and style. No more hiding, no more doubt, the shadow self was still present, yet had been silenced in silence, and even more so, my inner guidance was amplified. I knew I had gifts, knowledge and insight to offer others. Through an unlikely turn of events, the time frame of my plans shrunk as did my funding and I jumped forward regardless. When you say yes and commit to your true nature, you begin swimming with the currents of life. This signals to the powers beyond ourselves that have the ability to bend space and time if we have the courage to follow. I was on my way to a tropical island to begin creating and marketing transformational retreats.

The last 3 years of my journey in business and development, from then till now, has not been linear, yet business and life rarely is. It tends to be more like the way the constellations in the sky connect, you don't know they are until you know what you are looking at. I have experienced unexpected setbacks, perceived failures and financial stress. I have followed my inner compass into the complete unknown releasing my attachment to the how. I have had the opportunity to face even more of my own inner demons and doubts as I develop my writing, transformational programs, consulting strategies and marketing solutions. As I take on more clients and expand my capabilities, I experience levels of stress that I did not know existed. I have accepted that stress is a natural part of business and is an indicator of growth. To manage stress, I have developed healthy daily habits and rituals to help me combat its effects. I strengthen my body to process the stress I experience, making self-care a top priority. I have surrendered to the fact that there are times, if I shut up and listen, I am meant to let go of that which does not serve me even when I don't understand and time has its own plan.

When I connect to silence I receive exactly what I need to move forward. At times this is a kick in the butt, a message of patience, soothing reassurance or a shift in perception. I have also realized that sometimes it is not only what you do in business and life that creates your results but also what you don't, what you release and let go of; relationships, clients, beliefs or habits. There was a period of intense development that I cut out all unnecessary relationships and substances and I set the intention to everyday shut up and listen to my inner compass. Every morning for over a six-month period I rose with the sun to shut up and listen for the guidance of the day that emerged from within, wrote it down and shared it socially. During this time, I attracted abundance in multiple areas of life with ease and grace. I released my will to force outcomes, increased my patience and began to allow the natural evolution of my businesses free of personal judgement. I always follow the compass and take action even if I do not understand why. I have complete faith and trust in the support of the Divine and fully embrace the unknown. I would like to share some of the most profound messages I received during that time. This guidance continues to allow me to move forward trusting the journey ahead with a loving heart. I share in the hope that these messages will serve you and speak to your entrepreneurial flame as they did mine offering you the courage and strength it takes to develop yourself as well as your business.

ABUNDANCE

Today and every day I am open to receive abundantly in all areas of life. There is more to abundance then finances, I am also open to receiving an abundance of love, support, feeling of freedom, positive energy, laughter, grace, encouragement, courage, strength, clarity, kindness, and all other gifts of the human experience. I am open to receive abundantly.

ALLOWANCE

Today I open my heart to allow. I am open to new experiences, opportunities, understanding, relationships, connections and feelings. I am willing to expand my current reality to included more of what serves my soul. I open my heart to align my vibration with that of my best self and welcome all that connects me to my vision. I am one with Source.

COMMITMENT

Today I recommit. I have set out a plan for my desired life, I know that it is a compounding effect of my daily efforts that bring my dreams into my reality. Today I recommit 100% to my creation, to my rituals and my supportive habits. All choices I make today are aligned with my outcome. I deserve all my desires.

COURAGE

Today I have the courage to see beyond the Illusion. I have the strength to search within to discover my truth. I release all the outer ideals and expectations imposed upon me. I am free to expose my inner vibrancy.

FEAR

Today I am freed from my fears and doubts. I free myself through expression. As I give myself permission to fear and acknowledge that it is a completely natural part of life, I am able to reduce its power over me. As I examine fear and doubt it gives me clarity on what my next life lessons are, because as I gain knowledge and understanding fear and doubt dissipate. I am safe and I am free.

EMOTIONS

Today I acknowledge that though I am here on an emotionally complex human experience I am not defined by my emotions. I allow my emotions to come and go like the waves of the ocean. My emotions do not define or control me for I know I have the power of choice. As I acknowledge how I feel, I am grateful for the colourful emotional experience of life and release. I consciously practice this cycle over and over throughout my days. I am emotional, but I am free.

EVOLUTION

I choose to see my life as a constant evolution. I am evolving into the best version of myself which appears to the human eye as change, though evolution is more like blossoming. I am constantly learning, growing, mastering and blossoming, just as flowers do. Just as flowers blossom, die and begin the cycle again, I follow that natural cycle. When I embrace the idea of it all being natural I am able to release my fears around change. I am able to embrace that which has shaped me, even struggle or pain. Struggle can be a key ingredient to evolution and that I accept.

GRATITUDE

I rise with the sun and find strength in a new day. I open my eyes and heart to the beauty that surrounds me and choose to be grateful for this life. As I am grateful for where I am, who I have in my life and what I have become, I know I am in a vibration of attracting more to be grateful for. I find strength within myself to be grateful for my challenges, as they show me how to discover my inner darkness and turn it to light, which is my unique mission.

HAPPINESS

Today I am reminded that no one and NO thing has the power to make me happy, only I hold that ability and responsibility in my life. I am accountable for my feelings and own them. When I try to be the source of others happiness or expect others to be the source of my happiness I only experience feelings of inadequacy. I choose my own happiness and know that when that is my focus others around me will be consumed by my happiness and if they are not that is them not allowing happiness into their lives. I choose my happiness now.

LOVE

Today I acknowledge my greatest gift to the world is how I love. The combination of how I love myself, others, the creatures of earth and Mother Earth are unique to me. It is through loving that I create the tapestry of my life. At times I may choose to love through guidance or shelter, through safety or encouragement, through a random act or kindness or a committed donation. At times love can be shown through pain or frustration, through stern words or seemingly harsh action. Though it is all love. I am a completely unique expression of love.

PEACE

Today I consciously choose to connect to my inner peace. It is through the belief in universal love and connectedness that I find peace. When I internally choose peace because I know that every aspect of my life is working for me, for my evolution, for me to become a fuller expression of my higher self, I can accept all aspects of my life and change my perspectives. I Am whole, I embrace my journey and I am free from any limiting ideas.

PERCEPTION

Today I choose to see my life as an impermanent state of perfection. Change and evolution are the only constants. I choose to find comfort in this rather than fear it. I embrace that life changes in ways I do not expect and I choose to look for the divinity in every experience, remembering to ask how can I see every change as an act of love on a grander scale then my current reality? Thus not only acknowledging the beauty in my evolution, but also expanding my current perceptions. I am impermanent perfection.

SUPPORT

Today I acknowledge that my experiences are revealing my beliefs. If there are patterns occurring in my life it is because that is what I am asking for, a part of myself I need to nurture or an area I must evolve. The higher powers are always supporting me and giving me 100% what I ask for. This means to create change in my life I must reprogram my beliefs to align with my hearts desires. I know that this takes time and I gift myself the patience that is necessary for my results to manifest. I know my life is changing because I am thinking different thoughts and taking different conscious actions that are creating a different reality. I trust the process, release the need to force outcomes and know that what I attract is the perfect for my journey.

TIME

Today I take a breath and remind myself that there is enough time in the day to accomplish all that is necessary. My ability to prioritize and organize tasks allows me to achieve far more then I expect and still have time to enjoy life. Along the path of achievement, I remind myself to take in each step as it unfolds and trust the process. I allow the support of a higher power into my life and know that I am never working alone. I am supported. I am capable. I am patient.

UNCERTAINTY

Today I make room in my heart for the unknown. It is ok to not have all the answers, to not know what is around every corner. I welcome the unknown even though it feels more natural to fear it. I acknowledge the fear and move through it, not allowing my motion to be stifled by it. Even if I let fear stop me, it is only a temporary pause to allow for a raise in awareness. Today I embrace uncertainty and move forward. I am the creator.

May these words give you courage and strength to move forward, to persevere in times of doubt, chaos and change. There is a love beyond all measure that is the connecting force of this life when you shut up and listen for its whisper during silence or shout during struggle.

Judy Lee

Being raised on a farm in northern Alberta, Judy was taught a strong work ethic and determination at a young age. With college education in Business and Office Administration she always felt that positive mindset and strong character served her purpose in the real world rather than the 'right' education.

With a highly motivated entrepreneurial spirit, love of marketing and business in general, Judy has successfully owned a home-based cake decorating business and also co-owned a busy cafe - understanding firsthand the struggles and prosperity owning a business can bring. She hopes her optimism and genuine love of life can bring inspiration to others.

judylee65@hotmail.ca

https://www.facebook.com/judy.lee

Chapter 13

Leap(s) of Faith

By Judy Lee

I can vividly bring back the feelings and memories of my last call taken while dispatching for the Royal Canadian Mounted Police in Red Deer, Alberta. During a spring snowstorm in 2002, around 6:00 in the morning a young gentleman had gone off the road in his vehicle, over the embankment and down into a valley. The roads were icy and snow covered, still snowing and very cold and windy. He called 911, I answered his call and he was frantic, he had a vague idea of where he was but nothing exact that would allow me to send an officer to help him. He was quite a distance from the highway as he could not see the lights of the traffic. I kept asking questions all the while, trying to assure him that all was well and we would find him and get him help. Throughout the conversation I was able to determine with the help of a map which road he was on and quickly dispatched the RCMP member to try to locate him.

I encouraged him to hike up the hill back to the highway where hopefully a vehicle would stop to assist him. He was not feeling at all positive about doing this but I kept encouraging him – he started the long hike up the steep hill. He was cold, I could hear his teeth chattering; he was out of breath and wanted to stop and go back to his vehicle to wait - "No, no" I said, "keep going, you can do this, you can do this. Someone is going to be there to help - you keep going!" He finally got back up the hill to the highway where the RCMP officer was waiting. The caller made it back up from the valley to the highway, and was so happy to see the RCMP officer that he hugged him right on the side of the road!

This whole process took approximately 45 minutes from the time of the call to where it ended, calling the tow truck to get the vehicle from down in the valley. The RCMP member called and talked to me afterwards and mentioned how grateful the caller was that I encouraged him up from 'the bottom of the valley' and that we had gone out of our way to help him.

This ended as one of the few 'happy' calls, as there weren't many 'happy' clients calling the RCMP but I knew in that moment that would be my last call as I had been having mixed feelings of moving on to do other things. Being responsible for my health and what went on in my life, I had to make the choice to let go of my position with the RCMP, and move on. It was a very difficult decision at the time but knew it was one I had to make for myself.

Being born and raised on the farm in a small hamlet in northern Alberta, our parents taught us to work hard, never give up and extend kindness to all people. Along with my older brother, we took our turn driving the tractor, feeding pigs, milking the goat, building and painting the granaries – there was always fun things to do. After school, I worked at the local grocery store, played all school sports, and had lots of friends. I had an extreme love of horses and would ride for hours on end when I needed to find some space. Living in a small rural area we knew everyone and everyone knew our family – neighbors helped neighbors, we curled and skied as a family, played hockey all in the great spirit of a close-knit community.

Looking for a summer job after Grade 11, I knew the pool didn't have a teacher so I went and talked to the owner – she said in order to teach, you have to have your bronze medallion and instructors training. I took the bronze medallion training from owner's daughter and went to another town 3 hours away on 2 weekends to complete the instructors training. I wasn't a very strong swimmer but enjoyed this opportunity that I created for myself.

After high school, I left for Grande Prairie Regional College where I obtained a diploma as a legal assistant and a certificate in business. I really have little recollection of this education as it was not a huge priority at the time. In years to come I discovered the training I had secured, then proved invaluable would come back to me at a time when I needed it most.

While living in Grande Prairie, I was hired as a switchboard operator at the local RCMP detachment. I worked the switchboard and in the records department for 2 years, and then transferred into the communications/dispatch center. This is where all the action was – it was very busy. I was always multitasking and I loved it. A few years later, after getting married and having 2 daughters, we were transferred to Red Deer. Working shift work when our kids were younger always seemed to be easier for the family – not as many day care days and one of us was usually home on the evenings and weekends.

However, as the kids got older the shiftwork, constant business and multitasking takes a toll and I started to think of other ways to make money. My sister in law suggested cake decorating – this got me very excited. – I looked into courses and ideas and I began planning and creating this business. I completed cake decorating classes in Edmonton and started doing cakes.

We moved to a smaller house, with a lower mortgage so that I could start a job share position – as some medical concerns were sending me in a different direction. - I made a commercial kitchen in the basement of this house, which was approved and licenced with the city and health department.

My beautiful new commercial kitchen - it was bright, had French doors, a big window, a convection oven, and was a joy – it was great to work in. I took orders over the phone, had clients come into our home and view cake books and sample cakes. I was busy year round, particularly in the summer with weddings.

I found a great recipe for carrot cake that had a creamy pecan filling between the layers and cream cheese icing – it was outstanding! I had found a signature item! I gave cakes away to friends, neighbors, teachers at the neighborhood schools – left a business card, and this was a great start to a great business. My phone started to ring for orders - I did a wedding show, gave away samples of cake and got orders for the summer. The first wedding I did was individual carrot cakes on each table – it was a big order – I felt like I had no idea what I was doing but it all looked great and was so much fun!

During this time, I was working a half time position in the dispatch center and eventually moved down to one third time. I knew my 16 years with the RCMP was coming to an end. I was having feelings of wanting to make a change but wasn't sure how or why to make the end. The money was good, I had a great pension, especially now with the job share I could work the days that I wanted but this was still overwhelming for me. I felt like I was trying to go up the down escalator or paddling my canoe against the current. Totally feeling out of my zone. If only I could find the courage to make the transition - I knew in my gut if I let go, something else would come along. I was unsure of what my future held, but my intuition told to me trust and have faith that everything would work out for the best. I left in June 2002, had a busy summer of making cakes for weddings and was just waiting for the next opportunity to come along.

I had a friend, Louise Zanussi, that made specialty chocolates as a home-based business. I didn't know her that well; I had met her at nursery school with our kids and knew her husband was an RCMP officer. I was helping her with chocolates before Christmas and asked her if she wanted to go into business together – maybe a café or something. I'm not sure where this came from and why I would ask her this – but as the saying goes 'like attracts like' and we had no idea what this really meant for us.

A few weeks later I was talking to a friend that worked in the Millennium Center downtown and she mentioned the café in the building had closed down. I instantly knew this was my next project. I didn't know 'how' this was all going to work out but absolutely knew this was the 'what' I was looking for. After going over details with Louise we both felt very motivated to pursue this new venture – not really knowing why – but proceeded with full force.

We jumped in, writing up the proposal for purchasing this bankrupt business. We had quite a few roadblocks in our way – endless calls to lawyers and management of the building, searching out information and, many banks not wanting to lend money to female entrepreneurs buying a bankrupt food service business. After countless phone calls, analyzing a lengthy lease, and crunching numbers we submitted our proposal on December 15, 2002 and it was accepted! With money from our personal line of credit and a great deal of enthusiasm, we opened our doors January 22, 2003.

We had a very vague business plan, no partnership agreement but we a powerful knowing that this was going to work and we would have a lot of fun along the way. We had the best of both worlds in our personalities – Louise being strong with food, costings, baking, preparation work and the knowledge gained from previous experience in other food service establishments and myself with the business background, marketing, sales, administration and organizational abilities. Now was the time I could finally put to use the skills I learned at college. We were in the perfect downtown location, on the main floor of a 7-story office building so the proximity to target customers was perfect.

As our business grew over the years, it never felt like a job – it always was such a privilege to be there – this 'café' was an extension of our home with our customers and clients being felt as though they were our friends and family. We were busy – always busy – some days overwhelmingly busy - but we persevered through the bad days, staffing issues, sick staff members phoning in at 6:30 in the morning, last minute catering orders, missing stock on deliveries, and constant multitasking. Some days were really, really hard but kept to the powerful knowing that all is going to be okay. Sometimes just a good night sleep would take away the stress of the day and come morning would be ready for the next venture the day held. We also knew we had the support of each other and together we would work it out.

Louise and I had a sister-like relationship – we took turns being the glue that held things together while the other had a bad day. We loved helping the people – we extended kindnesses to our staff and customers. We tried to think of others and in our business and how could we help others in our community and in the world. We made trays of cookies for many, many fundraisers and donated often to charities. This friendship seemed to be 'arranged.'

I am usually very optimistic and try to remain positive - my main focus is on the positives, the blessings and the good fortune that this business gave us. I recalled a lot of negatives, bad days and unfortunate circumstances but they all remain very minimal in my mind and can instantly recall the grace this business delivered to both of us.

This business took us to places that we never dreamed possible. The financial reward was more than we had ever known, we were able to employ all of our children which eventually helped all four of them through university which was very helpful to our families. I think we both felt the money was just the bonus as we would have come to work anyways – this business was a gift that we treasured.

The business kept growing and growing with walk in customers and also daily catering during the lunch hour. It felt as though we just opened the doors and the people came, the phone rang, and the opportunities kept coming. We always seemed to know what to do next. We loved to help the people.

During my last few years in business I was starting to have feelings again that it was time to move on and try doing something else. The same kind of feelings that brought me into this business were now making me feel like I should move on. I wasn't liking who I was becoming – always exhausted, not wanting to get up and go to work, easily frustrated and anxious and I found myself pulling away when things got chaotic. As much as I loved the work, I didn't like what it was doing to my body.

I tried to push those feelings away; I loved my job, I loved the business and I could never leave – that was crazy! However, sometimes, at the end of the day I would just sit in my car and wonder 'how much longer can I do this?' Immediately, the other side of me would say 'how can you leave? How will our family manage financially? How would they ever run the business without me? What will the people say? What will I tell the people? What will I do with my time?' I kept going, pushing down those feelings and struggling with exhaustion through the days.

Our oldest daughter Brittany worked at Sunreal Property Management office downtown, close by to where our café is situated. The general manager of that office, Mike Stevens was a previous manager of the Millennium Center – he became like a friend as we got to know him fairly well – we took their family a care package when a family member was having surgery, and he helped us in negotiations when we were having a problem with our lease. One day on my way home from work (at this time I was only working until noon) I had to stop by her office and drop off some mail, I put together a small lunch for her and thought I would make a small tray of pumpkin cookies for her to give to Mike.

My daughter texted me right away after delivering the cookies to Mike and he was so surprised and grateful to have them. He then proceeded to give her a $50.00 bill to give to me to purchase a gift card from our business to give to his son who is going to the Donald School of Business which was in the same building as we were in. His son was very well known to our staff as being very friendly and always stopped to chat.

The circle of a random act of kindness. This was a huge 'divine' moment for me – I instantly felt warm from the top of my head to the tips of my toes. My brain immediately told me that I would never find a job again that would give this type of fulfillment – where most of our customers were like friends and family and I had the freedom to be my own boss. I should have been more thankful and grateful that I could experience this type of encounter with one of our customers through our business. How could I ever think of leaving this type of personal gratification that I received from this incident? This was outstanding and I needed to change my thoughts about leaving. We just never really know how a smile can change someone's day or in my situation how the reciprocation of kindness can reinforce a feeling and help to make changes in our lives.

After this experience, and during the Christmas break (we always took off the time between Christmas and New Years – another perk of being in business for yourself!). I reflected a great deal on this occurrence through my daughter. Towards the end of that week I realized this encounter wasn't a sign to hold on to what I had, but a reason to let go – this business was a blessing in my life in so many ways and even in letting go all things would be okay. The personal success that I had experienced in the business would carry on to other areas in my life. I needed to trust my intuition, let go and have faith – so hard to do when you like to have all the control.

After the new year, I found the courage to have the difficult conversation with my partner about leaving the business, and made the plan to be finished by the end of April 2016. I had no focus as to what I was going to do but knew I needed to take the time to take care of myself. Looking back over that time I can now see the signs that I was ignoring – long recovery from a minor surgery, inflammation in my body, exhaustion, headaches, insomnia, vertigo – all of these encouraging a lack of balance in my life.

This whole process pushed me out of my comfort zone to a place where I did not want to go - acknowledging and dealing with my own emotions and also dealing with the loss of this amazing business that we had created and I would no longer be a part of. Perhaps it was easier to push aside those feelings at the time than to really become responsible for what was going on in my life and how it was affecting my body.

As I reflect over the times in my past that I overcame fear and apprehension to create change, I am reminded of the gentle nudges of re-direction that I have experienced during critical moments. During the occasion when, as a young RCMP dispatcher, I was fortunate to be the one that answered the call of that young man who careened over the embankment and found himself at the bottom of the valley. His frantic request for assistance, and my part in encouraging his climb to the top, was a gift that triggered my own search. I too was searching for a way up out of my valley of perceived safety, which stunted my growth, limited my purpose, preventing flight to new horizons and opportunities. The gift of being the one to inspire and motivate that young man to find higher ground intensified my need for change, and greater purpose in this life.

Looking back, I understand now that I was limited and challenged by my fear of the unknown, fear of rejection, and a comforting false illusion of safety in sameness. In retrospect, I realize that had I listened to my intuition, and trusted my feelings demanding change earlier, great opportunities were waiting. As with my role during that last RCMP call, providing inspiration and motivation, I am becoming responsible for climbing that hill to create awesome change in my own life. I will continue my journey sharing optimism, kindness, and experiences gained during my 'leaps of faith,' to motivate and assist others as they navigate their journey up out of their valleys.

Sometimes this time spent in the valley helps us find our authentic self. A place where we can monitor awareness in our lives and links to our true selves - living a life with grit. Be responsible for living a life with true passion and love. Be aware, live with passion, share your light.

Noelle Leemberg

Noelle is an international speaker, trainer and certified business coach. Her passion and purpose is to help entrepreneurs increase their net profit percentage while preparing the business to run without them, so they can live the life they want. She uses the Forzani Business Coaching Program, developed from many failures and successes prominent Canadian entrepreneurs experienced building multimillion dollar business'. Her innate ability to connect and inspire others, along with her vast business experience and growing knowledge enables her to drive results for her clients. She is a problem solver; a connector and is insightful in the world of business.

Website: www.bSavvy.ca

Chapter 14

Dispelling 7 Misconceptions in Business

By Noelle Leemberg

Just because you can bake a pie doesn't mean you can run a bakery. Being great at your chosen profession is only the beginning to building and sustaining a successful business. And by successful, I mean a business that is predictably profitable and will one day run without the you, the owner. Building a business takes a certain type of person. Someone who lives by *The Optimistic Creed*, is incredibly determined and courageous, willing to continuously learn and evolve and do whatever it takes to overcome the many obstacles that occur. There are a number of core competencies and skills required to run a business. A business requires processes and systems that need to be implemented and made routine in order for it to thrive.

I believe in and support small businesses. They drive our local economies. Business owners have a great advantage; they can earn the life they want to live. Yet statistics tell us that many small businesses fail. According to the U.S. Small Business

Administration, 50% of businesses will go out of business by their fifth year. Industry Canada reports that 15% of all businesses fail in their first year. That number doubles to 30% by the second year and by the fifth year, 49% are no longer in business. It's time to change those statistics. Time to dispel some myths to increase the likelihood of success for all the eager entrepreneurs.

After working with a number of small start-up business' that failed and small business' that became extremely prosperous, I gained an understanding of why the various companies experienced the result they did. I worked for a recycling company in 1995 who wanted to be an industry leader, bringing recycling to condominiums and apartment buildings but their lack of planning caused them to shut down within a year. In 2000 just before the dot com crash, I did research and sales for a software and technology company hoping to optimize the operations of golf courses. The vision wasn't strong enough to overcome the market conditions, they didn't have a contingency plan and they went bankrupt.

In 2006, I was in a leadership role with a company who validated competence in the workplace using an incredible online tool with algorithms to assess one's abilities. The vision was clear but we lacked in planning and execution. Shortly after, I landed a role with an amazing privately owned company, led by a man with a vision that inspired the entire organization to follow his lead and make his dreams a reality. We did extensive planning. We measured the results of our actions, revised the plan and created systems and methodologies in every aspect of the business. We took the small company national and became an industry leader, winning numerous awards.

Experiencing success and failure many times as a business professional has led me to running a successful business coaching practice today. I made mistakes, had many misconceptions and experienced working in companies that didn't succeed as well as multimillion dollar organizations that are leaders in their field. That's why I know that what I am about to share with you is not B.S.

Myth #1 - Creating Your Vision Can Wait

Business owners love to work on strategies for their business. It's a common misconception to think that your vision is not as important as your strategies, here is why. Strategies are the 'how to.' How to increase revenues through sales, how to target the right audience with marketing or how to decrease your expenses as a percentage of sales.

The how, or the strategies you use to build your business are important, however developing your plans before creating your vision can actually block you from thinking big. If you don't build your vision first, then once you do, your 'how to' strategies may not be applicable. Time is a commodity you can't get back so it's more important to build your vision first. In simple terms, your vision statement is where you want to go, what you would like to achieve or accomplish. It sets a defined direction, a road map to your destination.

At the heart of every successful business is a concise and believable, clearly written vision statement. Take Whole Foods for example; their vision statement 'Whole Foods, Whole People, Whole Planet' is effective at showing the desired future state of the business. The first part, 'whole foods' describes what exactly they are offering product wise. The 'whole people' component of the vision statement shows that the company wants to be successful in supporting healthy lifestyles for everyone, from ownership to the employees and the communities they serve. In addition, the 'whole planet' component indicates that the organization aims for global leadership in their industry.

Your vision statement must align with your core beliefs and values so it creates a spark within you that fuels your purpose. A compelling and succinct vision statement will open up new opportunities, drive your ambition, your optimism and create momentum for your business. It will help you when you feel overwhelmed, burnt out and are working through the many challenges that entrepreneurship presents. Overall, a clear vision statement leads to understanding of where you want to go, which leads to making more impactful decisions, doing effective activities and this leads to greater results for you and your business. Aren't great results what you are striving for?

Myth #2 - Improvise and Wing It!

In 1993, I was backpacking in SE Asia after five months in Australia and New Zealand where I decided to stay a little longer, ok a lot longer. I cancelled all my prescheduled flights and decided to 'wing it' when it came to finding a flight home. I called the airline day after day, for a few weeks, hoping to book a flight back to Canada. I thought *no problem, I'll wing it when I get to the airport.* There I was, 25 years old standing alone in the airport in Kuala Lumpur with little money, an overstuffed backpack and no place to stay. The airline attendant told me there were no flights, not that day, or any of the coming days that week that would bring me home. Clearly my plan, or complete lack thereof, didn't work! A lesson learned on the importance of planning rather than winging it.

In business, it is critical to plan. Improvising only works in sales, service and at reception, not in the grand scheme of running a business. Planning helps an organization chart its course in the achievement of its goals. There are various types of planning depending on the size and structure of a business. Financial planning both short term and long term are critical to the success of the company no matter what size it is. Profit planning, aimed at generating a greater return, increasing market share and working to overcome any foreseeable problems. Strategic planning, a more systematic process usually used to create broadly defined objectives and actions to achieve them based on the vision. Succession planning to establish goals for talent management and the training required to develop experienced employees into valuable leaders. And of course, contingency planning. Remember when 'Plan A' doesn't work, there are 25 more letters in the alphabet.

Since planning is a core fundamental to business faring well, I recommend you spend a considerable amount of time working 'on' your business. At the beginning of each quarter, create a 90-day plan. This forces you to be proactive and productive at the same time. How? Using Stephen Covey's analogy of Big Rocks with a bit of a twist. Ask yourself what tasks are impactful to your income statement. Then figure out if they are urgent or important. Schedule blocks of time in your calendar to tackle these tasks first. If you don't schedule these in, they won't get completed because everything else that hits you throughout your day will appear to be more urgent.

Along with a 90-day plan, to really capitalize on your time, create a default calendar. Simply list all the tasks you do in a month. Categorize them and figure out how much time you need to spend on each task. Keep your timeframe tight, meaning- get really focused on each task so you can complete it quicker. Then slot those tasks into your calendar every week for an entire month and let the calendar manage you. Nearly every month will look the same except for those months where you do quarterly planning and budgeting. The benefit of using a default calendar, is you know exactly what you are doing at any time of the day. It keeps you focused, organized and allows your creativity to flow rather than using brain power to remember what you are supposed to do next.

To plan however, you need to think. To think you need time to yourself as well as time with your partners, shareholders and leadership team. Once again, the key is to schedule time to think in your calendar. Since planning is about managing your resources, your priorities and your activities to gain a higher net profit percentage, I'd suggest it is one component that needs a lot of attention. It's faulty thinking that you can improvise or wing it when it comes to running a healthy sustainable business.

Myth #3 - Pay Yourself Last

One of the most common misconceptions I see as a business coach is owners who chose to pay themselves last, if at all in some cases. Why does this happen? They don't include their fair market salary in their fixed expenses. Often this is due to a total oversight or understanding that doing a budget is essential to starting, building and growing a profitable business. Whether you purchase a business or start one, in most small businesses, the owner plays many roles. If you are a hair stylist and you run a salon, you must consider the two main roles you play. Your first role is that of a business owner because you have a responsibility to your staff and all the clients of the salon. Second is your role of the stylist. If your goal is to create a predictably profitable business that one day runs without you, you need to hire a general manager to run the business for you. This person will expect to be paid fair market salary. If this is not a line item on your budget, your business will not pay you the net profit percentage you plan for as you exit the company, whatever your exit strategy may be.

When you don't pay yourself first, you simply own a very stressful job.

Myth #4 - Do it Yourself

With hundreds if not thousands of tools available online to help and support small businesses today, it's no wonder why so many owners try to do everything themselves. From graphic design of their cards and brochures, building a website, managing the books, purchasing products, networking and selling, to the latest time consuming activity of managing an online presence on all the main social media platforms. You really could learn how to do all of these things but why would you? While learning and evolving is a love of mine and many others, learn and evolve in areas that match your strengths!

If you are an architect, engineer or an accountant, designing your marketing or selling may not be your strength. If you are a service provider in the health industry, budgeting and forecasting and managing the books may not be your strength and if it isn't a strength it's likely of little or no interest. All of the components of running a business are important if you want to reach great levels of financial success. The lesson here, is to outsource. It saves you time, energy and in the long run, money.

What many people forget, is that asking for help is not a sign of weakness, it is exactly the opposite. Asking for help is a sign of strength.

Business can be more competitive than professional sports. Professional athletes have many coaches. Why? Because they are focused on being the best and if you want to be the best you can be in your field, you need others to help you get there because the competition is intense. Think of your competition as more than just those who operate in the same industry. For example; If you operate a plumbing company and your specialty is creating home spas with steam showers, your competition isn't necessarily just the other plumbing specialists. It's the river boat cruise down the Amazon. It's the all-inclusive VIP tickets to the Super Bowl or the annual shopping trip on Fifth Avenue in New York City. You must be savvy to overcome your competition, and prosper in business.

Outsourcing, asking for help, hiring professionals and people smarter than you is essential to your success. If you think hiring a professional is expensive, try hiring an amateur which in some cases, may be you. Hire experienced people to help in the departments that are not your strengths. Hire a business coach. Your business will grow faster if you stop doing everything yourself and your spouse will thank you.

Myth # 5 - Sales is a Numbers Game

It's true, the more people you talk to the more people will buy from you. However, with sales people required to do more than just pick up the phone and talk to people, with high competition in the marketplace, consumer's expectations continually on the rise and pricing a part of nearly every decision making process, sales has become far more than a numbers game. This is now a myth. Sales is a game of professionalism. And it is both an art and a skill that takes many years to master.

It's essential that sales professionals know how to create harmonious productive relationships because people buy from people they like and trust. In 1993, the American Psychological Association published a report that found the most successful sales reps were 'conscientious.' This trait is found in people who take great pride in their efforts, are efficient, thorough and organized; who are vigilant and who care, about both their internal and their external customers.

A sales professional is respectful; of people's time, needs, wants, feelings and reputation. They have the desire to listen with an intent to understand. This means, they have the ability to shut up. They ask questions instead of selling and telling. Being energetic, willing to learn and having the ability to adapt are all a part of being coachable, a key trait for a professional. This ties in directly with a need for a positive attitude and sense of optimism. Nobody experiences more rejection than sales. Their drive and initiative makes them go getters. When they are disciplined and focused, persistent and passionate, personable and prepared, they will be a valuable member to any organization.

Some of these characteristics are innate, others are learned. Couple them with a killer sales process, expertise in their industry, the infrastructure and support of a team and a loyalty to their company, a quality product or service priced right and you have a super star. If you have a true sales authority, you will debunk the myth and realize that sales is about people and professionalism.

Myth #6 - Manage Your People

The challenge with this misconception is we have heard it for so long, we are convinced it must be true. In today's world of business however, people don't want to be managed, they want to be developed and led. Instead of managing people, we need to manage things. These things are systems, processes, and technology. Goals, standards and measurements. We need to manage a way of doing and directing. To build a successful business, we need these 'things.' They are the foundation.

Leading on the other hand is a way of being. Transformational leadership is a style of leadership that works with employees to identify the needs and optimize the operations of the business. These leaders guide change, improvement and growth through inspiration, engagement and authentic communication. Leaders support and develop their people, they share ideas and teach people to think, to take risks, be accountable and how to overcome their mistakes.

When you hire, keen professionals who aspire to be at their best every single day, ensure they are aligned with your beliefs, values and your vision. Then spend time with them (schedule this block of time in your default calendar). Develop them through training, feedback and generous recognition. Provide support, create a culture of authentic engagement and team work. To do this, help people understand through constant communication the goals of the company and how they are important in the achievement of the goals. People want to know that they are contributing. It makes them feel valuable. People are your greatest assets, develop them and your company will flourish.

When you have systems, processes and methodologies for people to follow and work with, you save time, energy, and money. Best of all, when mistakes happen, you can modify the systems. People like systems, it provides structure and guidance on how to do things well. Create a culture of purpose so people become more engaged in what they do. A more engaged workforce improves productivity and when productivity increases, costs decrease, revenues increase and you have a greater net profit percentage.

"Management is doing things right; leadership is doing the right things." - Peter Drucker

Myth #7 - Ask the Universe for What You Want and it will Happen

I am a big believer in the law of attraction, raising our vibrational energy and the power of the subconscious mind. Setting your intentions, managing your beliefs and doing affirmations is powerful and has merit. There is no B.S. in the fact that metaphysically speaking, we are all sources of energy, as are our thoughts and our actions. The challenge for most of us who are unseasoned practitioners in this field of science, is we only understand a small component of how the law of attraction really works. It is not as simple as ask and you shall receive. You can hope, dream, wish, want, and wait that your business to be successful but without executing on your plans, all the wishing and wanting will not get you to where you want to be. Especially if you don't believe in yourself, your work, or what you have to offer. If you have self-sabotaging thoughts or behaviors, some of which you may not even realize exist, you need to clear those before you can raise your vibrational energy and use the law of attraction to your benefit.

The point here is that you must take action in doing everything it takes to build and sustain a successful business. You must be aligned with your vision, have an unrelenting commitment to your company including your team and your customers. You must pay yourself a fair market salary. You have to plan in all areas of your business. Then create a default calendar to stay focused, on track and manage your behaviors so you can fit in the necessary projects and tasks that will help you gain the greatest results. Once you plan the work, work the plan! Learn the story behind your numbers and alter the plan to ensure the numbers are providing you with the net profit percentage you aim for. Outsource or hire the very best professionals to help you drive the business forward, develop and manage the systems and processes to ensure you have the foundation for predictably profitable business. Have a routine that you know works for you. Measure and monitor everything you do, every process you create, every number in your financials every month. Build an incredible team of dedicated employees, become a great leader, dedicate yourself to your company, your people, your customers and your community.

There is no B.S. in these seven misconceptions. Remember, knowledge without action is like having no knowledge at all. What is your burning desire? What are you going to do differently to help you build a highly successful, profitable business that will one day succeed without you?

Pam Robertson

Pam works as a coach, consultant, and part-time badass to help the flummoxed get more out of life and their careers. Her track record includes having developed more than 120 courses, collaborating on several international best-selling books, magazines including Be Fabulous at 50 and The Missing Piece. She recently launched the first two volumes in a series of journals for people and their dogs who like to write. You can connect with Pam on Twitter @PamRobertson, and benefit from her food and coffee obsession on Instagram, where she's @PamDRobertson.

Website: www.ladybirdfiles.com

Facebook: www.facebook.com/LadybirdsOnParade

Amazon: http://amazon.com/author/pamrobertson

Chapter 15

Would You Like a Side
of Lies with That?

By Pam Robertson

It's no wonder people still talk about sales and marketing as icky or unprofessional. I hear things like:

"Stick with me. I'll create a lead generator for $7 that'll bring you a kajillion clients."

"Once your website and all your social media accounts are fixed up, you can automate everything and do it in 15 minutes a day."

"Social media is amazing! It lets you market your business for free."

I was dipping my toes into the digital pond when my first computer could connect to the internet. Ten years later, I set up a pretty ugly little template of a website (though it was good for its time), and then waited for traffic. I was determined that my mom and my sister weren't going to be the only people finding me online, and I tried nearly everything I could.

The internet has completely changed our lives, and marketing has evolved along with it. We can reach more people now than ever, and we can target them with a huge degree of sophistication. This enhanced tracking and targeting ability is one thing that scares a lot of people away from digital spaces. Some even go so far as wishing a great spirit should simply guide clients to them and magically create a vibrant, profitable business. Personally, I think a lot of folks who are opposed to marketing have never learned what it can do for their business, or they haven't embraced what technology means, or they've been cheated through some underhanded shenanigans, and they are afraid. I feel like part of my purpose is to demystify marketing and make it understandable and useful to everyone.

There are plenty of great examples of what fabulous marketing has done. How do you think Tony Robbins can fill a stadium? How can J.K. Rowling sell so many books? Why do companies like Amazon or Walmart make money hand over fist, even when some products aren't of great quality? How is it that Google became the preferred search engine? They have all used using every marketing tool possible including television, live events, writing brilliantly and copiously, word of mouth, popup ads, guerilla marketing, referrals, affiliate marketing, and more. Of great importance, and not to be lost here, is that they also offer a product or service or price that the public *wants*.

There are a couple of singers whose work I love, and both of them arrived on the music scene at about the same time. Both are brilliant vocalists, though Michael Bublé has had way more commercial success and awards than Matt Dusk. When I look at their individual marketing strategies, I can see how things became so different for them. Bublé's strategy includes a very 'big' approach – he entertains, crosses musical genres from jazz into pop, and has created an enormous following through concerts, seasonal TV specials, and video. Dusk, on the other hand, has pointed his efforts to a narrower set of listeners who are committed to jazz and love the music for its own sake. He hasn't done the big TV specials or videos to the same level as Bublé, despite being a terrific artist and musical storyteller.

Tell Me a Story

I love stories. Do you? I like to read them, write them, watch them unfold on a stage or screen. One of the things that has huge influence on marketing's evolution is the way marketing leverages storytelling to get a message across. About ten years ago I met someone who taught storytelling as a way to share messages, and it had a huge impact on how I thought about strategy and the sharing of ideas. I have been very fortunate to attend classes and workshops in storytelling, drama, public speaking, and to have published stories that focus on writing to help share a message. Not that storytelling is the only thing you use in marketing and advertising, but it's a very important component.

If you recall people you've observed at a conference or through a documentary, the memorable ones weren't simply talking. If what they said compelled you to lean in and listen, and you laughed or cried, or started sharing with your friends, then you probably heard a story. Long or short, stories are the things we connect to. They stick in our memories.

People love stories, whether they are true or not (fiction or creative non-fiction can both create incredible stories), just as creative writing can. Many people naturally shy away from being sold to directly, but they quite easily tune into a story. Stories help persuade, and they help your messaging to stick. Marketing that uses a story has a lasting impact on people. When you craft your stories well, you can use them as part of your overall marketing strategy to connect with people who will come to know you, like you, and buy from you.

I love how marketing is evolving and that people and businesses are encouraged to be a lot more 'open' about who they are and what they stand for. This openness gets called different things, from being authentic, to connecting at a grassroots level, or growing your brand organically. Instead of representing their brand and being very formal, those who 'get' storytelling and authenticity are interacting in a more casual, down to earth way, even though it may be pre-planned and scripted. They share uplifting messages, incite laughter, and let an observer see who they really are, even without divulging all the 'dirty laundry.' They also share heartfelt, meaningful messages through storytelling, about the causes and issues that are important to them through their stories.

If you aren't sure of what I mean, put this book down for a few minutes or change the screen you are looking at to visit YouTube. Search for 'Budweiser Clydesdale commercials,' and see how each beer commercial tells a wonderful story that has an emotional tug. Yes, they are advertising their beer, and there is nothing wrong with that seeing as how commercials are intended to sell something. They just do it in a great way with stunning Clydesdale horses, and often a dog, cow, or donkey as well. Of course, story tellers go to much greater lengths than just leveraging cute animals. You can also search for 'Zappos beyond the box campaign,' or look for Kickstarter campaigns to see stories in action.

Sure, you can measure the value of clicks and conversions, and though it's harder to measure the value of connections you make it's not hard to figure out that as your presence, influence, and credibility grow, your business also expands. Most of that growth is because you are connecting with people who like something about you, and want to get to know you better. They like you, and they come to trust that you've got something they want or need (that's what we call the know, like, and trust factor). If you have enough of those people connecting to you and you have something good to offer them through a sale, then voilà, you're in business and people may just start remarking on your "overnight success!"

What's My Story?

I've done a lot of different things throughout my career, which means I do have oodles of stories I can draw from. There are good, funny, uplifting stories and there are poignant, sad, tear-jerking stories. Of course, you can't tell a story within your marketing and have it unrelated to what you are doing; that's the kind of marketing that makes people feel icky. But you can look at the situation you are in, and decide if you have a story to share that's going to help your message. You probably have loads of stories you can tell, brought forward from very normal parts of your life. Let me share a few with you.

My career path has been very twisty, rather than on upward trajectory. I'm not what you'd call a typical person in terms of where and when I have done things, and I like the term that Emilie Watnick uses for this: multipotentialite. It means that I am good at a lot of things, and I want to try lots of things out. I'm not tied to one career stream, and have worked in very different industries including the military, music, education, business, and culinary arts. My personality doesn't just allow me to dabble or work at an entry level in anything. I like to really dig in, and so I completed certifications and degrees in each of the areas I experimented in.

One unanticipated benefit of this approach has been a huge pile of stories I have collected over the years.

So, there's the time I was helping my sister move, and we were carrying a heavy dresser down the stairs. We were grunting and groaning and cursing – this was a highboy style dresser made out of maple and it weighed more than the two of us put together – when suddenly we made a horrible mistake. We looked at each other, right in the eye, and then began to giggle before we dissolved into full blown laughs, and I was laughing so hard that I lost my grip on the damned dresser and dropped it...on my sister! Thankfully, she wasn't badly hurt and she forgives quickly, but that dresser was never quite square in all the corners after that.

Another time I was speaking at a conference and had dutifully arrived early that morning to make sure the microphone worked in my presentation room. My turn came, and I was warming up the crowd when Robert poked his head in from the room next door and yelled, "Hey Pam! We can hear you in the next room." I paused and looked at him, "What, you need me to turn the mic down? It's too loud?" I asked. "You have to turn it off!" he explained, "you are hooked into the speakers of all the rooms on this floor!" Ugh! How embarrassing! Not only people who had come to see me could hear me, oh no, people who were trying to hear other speakers could only hear my presentation! I had to take my microphone off and use my best parade square drill sergeant voice to make sure I could be heard where I was.

Years later, I was driving across Canada with my son and my sister. We were relying heavily on a GPS in addition to paper maps (although this wasn't really that long ago, it was prior to any of us having Google maps on a smartphone). Somewhere in rural Ontario, we needed a bathroom break. My son programmed the GPS to find us a gas station, and about 30 minutes later (I mentioned we were somewhere in the midst of Ontario, right?) we were directed into a parking lot alongside a refinery. There was gas there, for sure, and plenty of it, but the only lavatory available was a patch of grass for the dogs to pee on!

Another time, I was teaching a class for career coaches in a dark hotel basement one day, and the organizers had ordered a really nice lunch. Unfortunately, I had an allergic reaction to something. Within just a few minutes of eating, my face swelled up, my eyes were puffy, and I had hives all over me! Fortunately, a friend of mine was there, and she ran across the street to buy me some antihistamine. I had to give the group an extra quarter hour to 'network' following lunch so I could let the drugs do their work, and then we carried on as if nothing unusual had happened whatsoever.

There was a time I dove off a diving board and the top half of my swim suit came off...and the time I was halfway up a majestic mountain, sneezed, and my horse bolted...and the time my car spun into the side of the massive High Level Bridge...and when I banged up my rental car in Ireland...and more.

Of course these stories all have some silly elements, but they can (and have!) been used to help me connect to people. They tend to get a few laughs from people who can relate to something that has happened.

As consumers, we become more demanding of great content in advertising, and so the sharing of a good story is no longer the domain of big name published authors. Storytelling is a skill that people need to master.

How to Give Your Marketing Efforts a Meaningful Upgrade

In addition to incorporating stories in your marketing, here are my top strategies to get your marketing working for you.

Collaborate

I'm a people person, and yet as someone who makes a big part of my living through writing, I also spend a lot of time alone. This is a perfect balance for me.

Since I don't have a large team that I work with (and since I lead that team), I frequently reach into my network for insight and collaboration. I feel very fortunate that so many colleagues and friends have trusted me with their personal numbers. These are influential people in the marketing space, and they are gracious with their time and knowledge, and I do the same favours for them in return. Reach out into your network. Don't take up too much of their time, be gracious, and be sure to return the favour in some way.

Get Some New Friends

If you're not hanging out with people who are better at marketing and storytelling than you are, then you need to find some new people. You can't have a business unless you market it, and if you keep doing the same old things or hang about with the same people, it's just a matter of time before you run out of things to talk about, plus you'll run out of people to speak with.

If you're someone who doesn't like the "buy me" and "shop here" yelling and screaming kind of marketing, you'll love how advertising in the digital space is changing. It's really become a case of share, help, and give. The 'buy here' button is replaced with 'send me the report' or 'send me my gift' or 'sign up to see the video' because we know that our customers don't want to be sold to; they want to learn, or be entertained, or invited, but they do not want to feel like the only thing you ever do is sell to them.

Get Organized

This point might seem harsh, but you must stop letting distraction, overwhelm, or a lack of decision making mess up your results. If you can't focus with your internet browser turned on and email notifications binging, then turn them off. If people are interrupting you, turn off your phone or close the door.

If you've told yourself that your situation is unique and you absolutely must be available 24/7 and you can't turn off your phone, consider this paragraph as me calling you out on your bullshit. Sure, there might be the odd occasion when you need to be available, or ready for a call, but that's what contingencies are for. If you are supposed to be working on a project for a client and you need to get it done, then stop playing games, or tweeting, or staring off into space waiting for inspiration to strike.

Set up systems that work for you and get back to business, and get the work done.

There is no Free Ride

When it comes to your marketing, there are lots of inexpensive tactics you can employ, for sure. Social media updates, press releases, blogging, bookmarks, text message campaigns don't have to cost a lot individually. However, they still take time and effort to produce and there is cost to that. They also need to be well written, incorporate your story, and that kind of good writing takes time and effort.

The bigger cost to your business, however, is that focusing on individual marketing tactics miss the point. Dedicating yourself to Facebook, for example, just because your market seems to be on Facebook doesn't mean that your marketing is going to work there. You must decide what you want to do (get people to click on something for a download, or join your list, or share your stuff), but each thing they 'do' is the result of a tactic. Step back and develop your marketing *strategy* first, then decide what activities or tactics will support your strategy and be clear with yourself that if a tactic doesn't support the strategy, you aren't doing it. Just because it's great to be on Facebook, or Instagram, or whatever your social media darling happens to be, it's not of value to you if your people aren't there and they aren't engaging with you.

Strategy wins. People love stories. If your strategy includes connecting with people through storytelling, then get writing some great stuff that helps them get to know you, your company, and what you stand for or against.

And, if you don't like to write and don't want to learn, gather writers around you who can take your stories and turn them in to something people will read.

You can do this.

ReeJade Richmond

ReeJade J. Richmond is a sought after business and leadership expert. She graduated from Albany State University with a B.S. in Criminal Justice and a Minor in Psychology with a Juris Doctorate degree. After achieving her law degree, ReeJade was blessed with a job at a world-renowned celebrity law firm where she worked on many exciting projects. But after some soul-searching, ReeJade discovered her true calling and founded Search for Her Existence, LLC and Leadership for Women (nonprofit). She helps women discover their greatness, personally and professionally. Her goal is to create a generation of one million women leaders before she dies. ReeJade currently resides in Michigan with her beloved husband and daughter.

Website: www.searchforherexistence.com

www.leadershipforwomen.org

Chapter 16

Learn from the Past, Live in the Present, and Lead into the Future

By ReeJade Richmond

I do not know about you, but I have been taught some straight 'bullshit.' If explicit language offends you, then you may want to skip this chapter. If you are a brave soul who wants to face truth, reality, and transformation, then keep on reading!

Once upon a time there was this black girl from the hood of Dayton, Ohio who was taught that education was king. She was taught that an education was her only way out of the hell she was currently living. She studied really hard. She got a full ride scholarship to attend undergraduate school. After graduating she went on to law school. Once she completed law school she found a job, bought a dog, found a husband, had a baby, and bought a house. Sounds like the American dream, right? Guess what? *Wrong!* This foolery I was taught left me in debt, depressed, and miserable. I was having at mid-life crisis and I was in my 20's! I was taught a lie. I was taught the bullshit way of living! If I continued living the way I was living I foresaw myself either committing murder or being buried six feet under very soon! So I decided to do something crazy.

I JUMPED.

I left any thought of rationality behind. I decided to leave my current legal position at a world-renowned celebrity law firm and took a leap. I was miserable and I desperately needed something to save me. I needed to work for myself. The problem with this notion is that I had not the slightest clue of what to do. All I knew is that law was not my intended purpose. I prayed, I cursed, I checked out. Then one day as I was driving it slapped me silly. I had an epiphany! I enjoy helping and mentoring women. Over the years at the law firm, many women tended to reach out to me for guidance and support during their tenure at the firm. When I was helping these women I would get a 'happy high.' As I reflected on this epiphany I began grinning from ear-to-ear like I was going on a first date. So I said to myself, this is it. I am going to teach women how to complete bad asses! In professionally correct terms I will help women be great personally and professionally. I hit the ground running. But of course the fairy tale could not be roses and sunshine.

THERE WAS TROUBLE.

My husband was not particularly happy with my abrupt decision leave my job. In fact, our marriage was on the line because I was choosing to pursue my own happiness. I actually began questioning my decision and what was important to me. I ultimately told my husband that my happiness was more important than his comfortability. We downsized, *a lot!* We were no longer living in the suburbs but on the west-side of Detroit. I convinced my husband that this was a temporary situation; that this was a blessing. We were living way over our means. In plain terms we were living paycheck to paycheck.

I HIT THE GROUND RUNNING.

I began developing my business. At the time I only had $100. I took $50 and established my LLC. I then got my tax id and opened a bank account. I placed $25 in the account. I then used the remainder to purchase a domain name and business cards. I was well on my way to helping women become bad asses!

Then there was a wall. I had no clue on what I would offer and what to put on my website. I began looking for other women who decided to hang their shingle as well. I came across an online women's entrepreneurial summit, hosted by the Women CEO Project. I learned a lot of tools to get started and I also befriended many of the attendees. I was moving and shaking. I was the cheerleader of my business. I wanted everyone and their mamas to know about my business.

I talked to everyone, I mean everyone. Then I hit another wall. I was not making any money. I went back to the drawing board. I asked friends and other business coaches what they thought about my business overall. I got an answer and I did not like it. My vision was not clear. My business did not effectively articulate why people should pull money out of their wallets for me.

I revised and revamped everything and the money began raining from the sky. But, I started feel drained and unhappy again. I spoke with a coach and I realized I was experiencing issues because I had not identified my ideal client. I was accepting any and everybody for a dollar! I started to become picky with my clients. I raised my prices and changed my payment policy. Once I did this something crazy happened; I started getting *more* clients.

LESSON 1: Use your past as a catalyst to do *epic shit!*

After three years of running a successful business, I got another crazy idea! I wanted to help *all* women; not just the women who could afford me. I then birthed the Leadership for Women movement. It was initially an idea to provide free leadership development resources to women globally. The overall goal was to create a generation of one million leaders. I started with a free virtual online summit in September 2014. During the summit we kept crashing the servers. We had to continue purchasing bandwidth in order for people to join.

I then began reflecting on my success and the feedback the summit received. I decided to turn Leadership for Women into an organization, but I did not know exactly what yet. I went on and hosted a live event Detroit, Michigan. The event sold out which what I expected, but there was one huge problem. Only 25 people showed up but the event was scheduled for 150 women. I later discovered that a sponsor purchased a large number of tickets but had not gifted them. I was embarrassed and defeated. I was ready to throw in the towel. But that crazy bitch of a person in the back of my head said *keep going.* A month after the summit I decided to evaluate and revamp. I hired a public relations professional and I decided to establish the movement as a nonprofit organization. I am pleased to announce that the next summit was sold out and we had actual bodies in seats! We were also sponsored by a major Fortune 50 company, Comcast!

LESSON 2: Learn to celebrate your wins and *live* in the now. Life will happen and that's ok.

Now I do not want to feed you a bunch of bullshit. To be an entrepreneur is hard work. It is pure insanity. As an entrepreneur you are constantly on a rollercoaster ride. I chose this lifestyle because I'd rather be the one giving myself heart attacks versus someone else. Every day is an adventure into unknown territory. As an entrepreneur I have been afforded something very valuable - *time*. I am able to spend time with my family when I want. I am also blessed with financial opportunity. It is all about balance. During the journey I have been diagnosed with stage four renal failure. I do dialysis three times a week as week as well as care for a special needs child. I just roll with the punches like Tyson!

LESSON 3: Do not place limitations on yourself. Start taking baby steps towards your fairy tale. You are the captain of your ship, begin *leading* it today.

I am always looking for ways to drive myself crazy. I am always creating new programs and events. I am always looking towards the future on expanding my vision to get that 'happy high.' I am like a crackhead looking her next fix on life. I am currently beginning endeavors into global expansion. I am really focused on creating a generation of one million women leaders.

If there is anything that I can leave with you it is this:

- Never settle for anyone else's bullshit. Your life is not meant to make others comfortable. Stop asking for permission to be happy. Just begin pursuing it vigilantly.

- You have to be willing to accept a new reality for yourself. Once you have done this you must begin to define the terms of this reality.

- You must be willing to fail. Your business, straight out the gate, is not going to be perfect. It will never be perfect. Instead you should focus on constantly evolving your business.

- Align yourself with other bad asses. I am not talking about the people put a lot of fluff on social media, but the ones who are really making money. Do your research like you are the FBI!

- Enjoy the process. Entrepreneurship will teach you a lot about yourself. Be humble and try to learn from every experience on your journey.

Now, I *command* you my grasshopper! Go out and do epic shit and do not take anyone else's bullshit but your own!

Susan McInnes, CPA, CGA

Susan McInnes, a chartered professional accountant (CPA) and owner of S. McInnes & Associates Ltd., has been in the accounting profession for close to 20 years. After many years of working in accounting firms and obtaining both her Bachelor's degree in Commerce and Accounting Designation in 2014 Susan purchased her own firm in 2015. In addition to being a mentor with the Chartered Professional Accountants Association Susan also volunteers her time with the CPA Financial Literacy program holding workshops to help individual and small business owners better understand their finances.

Facebook – www.facebook.com/smcinnesandassociates

Website – www.reynen.net

Twitter - @smcinnes25

Chapter 17

You Have to be Selfish
to be Successful.

By Susan McInnes

In my years as a professional student, employee and now business owner, I have come to understand the role that selfishness plays in success. Selfishness? That negative characteristic understood as being egotistic and consumed by self-centredness? Yeah that.

I can honestly say that owning my own CPA firm was never something I planned to do, certainly nothing that was an earlier obsession. Like so many of the decisions I've made over the years, developing S. McInnes & Associates Limited was based on a reaction to specific circumstances.

Fifteen years earlier I was a single mother of two young children; I'd recently left an abusive relationship and decided to return to school. It was a big step, and not easy, but it meant I was able to leave a bad situation, get myself off of welfare and provide for my kids. During this time, I completed both my Bachelors Degree in Commerce as well as my Certified General Accountants designation. I also met my husband during this time and he, along with my kids, have been a huge support system. Always supportive of all of my crazy ideas.

While completing my education I had worked in three different professional accounting firms. Each offered both job security and good future prospects, and in the case of one, the chance of becoming a partner with the firm. However, none of those opportunities panned out. In each of the firms my career objectives were not aligned with the needs of the partners of the firms. I left each of these companies for various reasons, I didn't quit however. Quitting carries such a negative tone to it – rather I fired my bosses for not considering my future aspirations. Firing your bosses is much more empowering than quitting a job.

In the case of one firm, it was my age that proved to be the factor; they were looking for younger students who could, presumably, commit to a long-term employment relationship with the company. I didn't match that criteria even though I was not yet 40. I chose to be selfish and left the firm. My future obviously wasn't going to be with that firm so I chose to not waste any more time with them and moved on. If they wanted youth and not experience why waste any more time with them.

In all three of these firms I encountered senior managers or partners who were not only insecure in their positions, but were threatened by anyone who dared to expose their weaknesses. By definition, they had become bullies. My work was constantly scrutinized by these individuals. In one firm, unjust scrutiny on the job went beyond the work environment, eventually descending into personal vindictiveness. I was accused of lying to them, and even had one partner go behind my back to try and catch me lying in order to discredit me to the other partners. On top of that, I was blamed for errors that I didn't make, all in an effort to cover up the mistakes of others. As I have found, bullying occurs in the workforce just as much as in other settings. I found myself in a position of constantly fighting to prove my worth and prove that my work was correct and that I did know how to do my job and that I did it quite well. I began to realize that I really didn't make a good employee as I wouldn't just sit back and take all the B.S. handed to me by those in charge.

A few months after obtaining my accounting designation I was offered a partnership with the firm where I worked at the time. Finally, it seemed, all those years in school had paid off. To say the least, I was thrilled; not only that, it was an achievement I would realize before reaching the age of 45. I would no longer be an employee and put up with the bullying that was occurring. At that point, life was great!

Two months down the road I had the offer stripped away; I was told that I wasn't ready to be a partner. It was a crushing disappointment but I believed they were being honest with me and believed I was not ready to become partner. I took what I thought were the necessary steps that would enable me to move upward and onward. Sadly, I didn't or couldn't see that due to the one partner's attitude towards me, I would never be able to realize that goal and consequently would never become a partner in that firm. During those few months I'd focused on bringing in clients while looking for different ways to generate revenue. I was determined to prove that I was partner-worthy; I'd even approached a firm where I'd once worked 20 years earlier in an attempt to obtain some consulting work. The owners of that firm offered a partnership to either myself or the firm I was currently working in. Still convinced I was not ready to do something like this on my own, I took the offer back to my employers – who promptly rejected it. At this point, it was obvious that this was an offer that I needed to pursue on my own and I started that process.

During my next performance review with my employer at the time, I was hit with another crushing blow: not only were none of my efforts recognized but instead I was told that I dressed too conservatively, that I was a good looking woman with a nice body, and I needed to show it off more. Really? I had spent months bringing in new clients and increasing revenue for the firm to prove that I was ready to take on a partnership role and now I was learning that all I had to do was show a little more skin. I was disgusted. After taking ten years to obtain my accounting designation I was no longer willing to put up with being taken advantage of.

All my years of training involved obstacles many would have found almost insurmountable, and that evaluation was the last straw! I had spent 10 years in school. Preparing assignments from a bench at the playground so I could still spend time with my kids; spent every Saturday morning at the library preparing for exams and even prepared an assignment from a hospital bed after having my gall bladder removed. I wasn't about to have all this effort cheapened by one partner's opinion. My ability as an accountant has nothing to do with how I dress or how much of my body I show off. At this point I realized that if I wanted to be a partner in a firm I would just have to build my own firm.

While letting go of the need to prove to them that I had the stuff to be partner, I started to realize that I could reach my goal on my own. Which, I did! I purchased the firm that had been rejected by my previous employer on my own as well as opened up a separate office location in Duncan, BC, the town where I currently live.

Now, as the owner of my own business, I am faced with a different set of challenges. It has definitely been challenging getting to this point, but my challenges are far from over.

Operating two offices that are 250km apart presents a challenge in itself, especially when all of my staff are in my out of town office. My time is now spent between the two offices and each week I am away from home for a night or two. Even though my kids are older and no longer in school this new business definitely takes me away from them and my husband much more.

It has been a challenge changing from an employee to a business owner. As an employee my basic responsibilities were to show up for work on time, do my job well and then collect my paycheque at the end of each pay period. Now I am not only responsible for doing my job but also ensuring we keep clients and obtain new ones. I am no longer just responsible for myself; I have employees who have families that rely on a paycheque from my company as well. If I fail, it's not only myself and my family that will be affected. It's a lot of pressure. So how do you keep growing and expanding? Marketing. It's is not as simple as one would think.

As a business owner, everybody wants a piece of the pie and everybody wants to sell you something. Which are the best marketing techniques? Where is the best place to spend the advertising budget? There is no quick or magic answer. It is simply trial and error and having offices in two different locations means having two separate markets to target. Marketing trial and error costs money and may or may not give you a return on that investment.

I was fortunate enough to purchase an established business which already had a very good reputation and was well known in the community. I also retained experienced staff, already proven to be loyal and reliable. Purchasing an existing business with existing staff was a challenge as well since the business was successful due to the staff who had developed a relationship with the previous owners. I was instantly faced trying to develop a relationship with the staff in order to retain them. Although one of the previous owners has remained with the company, instantly I was faced with the challenge of building and maintaining a good working relationship with the them as I didn't want to lose any of their services. It was not only the staff that I needed to build trust with and develop a relationship with but with the existing clientele as well.

As an accountant, the nature of my work is to deal with the finances and personal lives of our clients. This means developing a trusting relationship with your clients. In purchasing this business one of the founders of the company retired and I did not want to lose the client base that he had built up. Simply purchasing an existing business does not guarantee success or guarantee that you will have the same success. Clients may just decide to go elsewhere.

For me time management proves to be a never ending challenge. As an employee I would arrive, ready to begin work at 8:30am and at 5:00pm I would leave both the office and my work. Suddenly the matter of time management became a force to be reckoned with as I struggled to control the number of hours I spent on the job. There is always something that needs to be done and I could spend 7 days a week at the office. I eventually began to realize that time management was closely intertwined with learning to delegate tasks – another new challenge.

As the owner I have many more responsibilities and tasks that I could easily do and do quickly. However, I need to let go of some of these in order to free up my time to do other tasks that only I can do. It is hard to let go and have someone else do it as they may not do it the same way as I would. Or I may not always explain how I want something done so it becomes a learning experience on both sides. Goes back to time management though. I could work 24/7 but obviously that wouldn't work for long so I need to decide what tasks only I can do and delegate the others.

As a way to keep sane and force myself to take a break from the office I am very involved in dragon boating. I also spend considerable time at the gym training for different goals I set for myself. In addition to maintaining physical fitness, these activities help keep me focused on what I am doing, whether exercising or working at my business. The work ethic I follow at the gym I translate to my business. When I put in hard work at the gym I see results, if I put in that same amount of work at the office I will see results as well. It also gives me a great way to burn off steam and relieve stress.

I will not pretend that past several decades have been easy; they haven't been but it is through the lessons learned during those difficult times that have made me the fulfilled person and the successful business woman that I am. It continues to be difficult but like they say: "if it was easy, everyone would do it."

One of the biggest things I have learned is that a lot of women in business treat other women in business differently. As I have found, some of them, when they reach a role of authority become quite insecure and threatened by other successful women and rather than empower each other try to bring the others down. Some of the best advice I was given along my journey was to remember the bad managers that I have had and not behave like them. The business world is still an old boys club and tough enough for women, we don't need to make it tougher by treating each other badly and not empowering one another. Another thing I have learned along my journey is that if you want something you have to go after it yourself. Nobody is going to do it for you and the choices that you make may not always be the most popular ones but you have to look out for yourself.

As a woman in business I am often faced with gaining the confidence of clients simply because of my age and the fact that I am a woman. In my last year of school, while working in a professional accounting firm, the firm landed a client that they had been trying to get for quite some time. A big client, that was given to me. After one initial meeting, the client decided to pull their account. Why? Simply because I was a student and it didn't matter that I had more than 15 years' experience behind me. The client did remain with the firm but it took the senior male partners to smooth the waters. I did develop a wonderful relationship with the client but I don't think the initial impression clients take away from a meeting with a woman are the same as that with a man. I find I am constantly tested by men in meetings and I think as professional women we have to work harder to gain the confidence of clients.

I wouldn't change anything about my journey to get to where I am at today. The challenges I faced earlier in my career have prepared me for what I am facing now and I learned some valuable lessons along the way.

Susan Whalen Janzen, B. Ed.

Susan was born in Calgary, Alberta. After graduating high school, she was a professional singer and recording artist for 17 years and was proud to represent the City of Edmonton as the first local 'Klondike Kate' for two years. In 1996 she graduated with a Bachelor of Education Degree and taught special needs children for six years. In 2003 she became a licensed realtor. To better understand and communicate with clients she attended the Introduction to B.A.N.K. workshop at the eWomen conference in 2015 and is now one of the first certified and licensed trainers in Canada.

Facebook: Susan Janzen, B.Ed. Edmonton Realtor

https://twitter.com/Suesellshomes

www.susanjanzen.com

Chapter 18

Be Still

By Susan Whalen Janzen

"With every thought you think you are creating your present and your future." -Louise L. Hay

I've always had a heart for those who feel like they're on the outside looking in, for people who just want to belong and to be a part of something bigger than themselves. Even though today I am blessed with a loving husband and a fulfilling twenty-eight-year marriage, have five loving and accomplished children and eleven amazing grandchildren, and have a successful career, those feelings of wanting to belong still creep in every once in a while – just to remind me where I came from and to give me an opportunity to practice what I've learned about the gift of stillness.

To better understand where I am today as a business woman, it is important for you to understand where I came from. Since 2003, I've been a residential realtor in Edmonton, Alberta, Canada. Prior to that, I received my Bachelor of Education degree and was a special education teacher and taught for six years. Before that, and just out of high school, I was a professional singer. I sang throughout Canada and the USA for seventeen years. I wanted to follow in my mother's footsteps, because as a child, singing was all I knew.

My mother was raised in an orphanage and to be able to sing, although not lucrative, was a gift that she was blessed with. When she was just eighteen, in 1954, I was born. I know my mother loved me, but she didn't know how to be a good mother because she'd never experienced that herself. I was a baby out of wedlock, a 'love child,' or legally branded as 'illegitimate.' I was very aware of this stigma and always felt different. I was the only one of my peers who didn't have a 'typical' family: a father, siblings, or a family home. I felt like I didn't belong or fit anywhere.

Those feelings of being different started early. I lived with my mother off and on, and only when she felt she could financially support me. My mother suffered from depression but her intentions were always to keep me safe; but that didn't always happen. I attended a total of twelve different schools growing up, and although I don't remember all the places I lived, I do vividly remember the abuse that I received in two foster homes when I became a ward of the government in 1959. I was five years old.

In one of the foster homes, a teenage boy sexually abused me for eight months until I had the courage to tell my mother. Mom couldn't get me out of that house fast enough. Unfortunately, I was then placed in another foster home but no one paid much attention to me, until one sad day.

At the time, one thing I really liked about myself was my long hair. That awful day my foster mom said she was tired of brushing my hair and she cut it all off. I was terrified and felt invisible. I still remember the nightmare I had for years after that.

It was always the same; a monster was chasing me and I kept trying to run home but caught before I could make it. I always woke up in a sweat.

When I started grade one, I came out of foster care and moved in with Mom for a couple of years until we moved from Calgary to Edmonton, Alberta. She accepted a singing job to co-star on a weekly television show on CBC with Tommy Banks called Somewhere There's Music. Mom finally had her first opportunity at a steady income and it was an exciting time for both of us. Unfortunately, this lasted only a few months. Since Mom felt that she couldn't care for me properly, she placed me in The O'Connell Institute, an all-girls convent in Edmonton. I lived there for two and a half years with about 100 other girls, mostly orphans or wards of the government, who ranged in age from two to eighteen. The Sisters of Charity ran the convent and all six nuns must have been overwhelmed with the task of caring for so many children. My way of coping with each and every change that I experienced, was to be still and to focus on the positive things that I wanted to happen.

Until the convent, my strongest memory from each place that I lived was sitting and waiting for my mom to take me away. I never knew if or when that would happen and I was lonely and in a constant state of anxiety and fear. When I turned ten, I was diagnosed with irritable bowel syndrome (IBS). I was anxious about making new friends each time I moved, about when my mom would come to take me away, and if I would ever meet my father. I prayed that my mom would marry so we could all live in one place and I prayed for a large family. My deepest wish was to feel that I belonged.

While I was at the convent, something changed. Mom had told me about God and taught me to pray, but when I came to the convent

I was given a Catholic prayer book, with a white ivory cover! Since I didn't have a lot of my own things, I read it and cherished it.

This was also a time when I learned about responsibility. When I turned ten the nuns assigned me what they called a 'charge.' She was a two-year old girl named Karen. It was my job to get her up and dressed each morning, take her down to the cafeteria for breakfast before I went to school, to play with her after school, take her down for dinner, and to bathe and put her to bed each night. Actually, looking after Karen was something I loved to do.

When I was feeling sad, however, I would slip away and sit alone and still in the chapel with my prayer book. My prayer was always the same; I asked God for a dad, a large family and a house where we could all live. When we had Benediction the music I heard made my heart soar and I forgot all the bad things. I can still see the stained glass windows and smell the incense. It was the first time and place that I didn't feel afraid but really felt safe. Sitting alone and being still finally felt ok.

While at the convent I came to understand that although I did not have an earthly father I did have a heavenly one who was always there and who I could talk to anytime. Mom had instilled in me that I was very special but it was not until I was in the chapel that I felt special. I believed and had faith that my prayers would be answered. Some day. Like a security blanket, my faith covered and comforted me and gave me hope.

Even with this hope, I was still just a little girl who felt like an outsider. I did well in school academically but I tried way too hard to make friends and to fit in. I was bossy and always asked to be included rather than waiting to be invited. I was talkative and was always trying to get attention. Now that I'm older I understand how and why, instead, I pushed people away.

When I started Junior High I was living with my mother again, but feeling more like the parent than the child. This filled me with anxiety, so at age fifteen, when I finished Grade 9, I left home and moved back to Calgary on my own. My mom had taught me how to be 'street smart,' so I was confident and knew that I would be ok. I was, however, very determined not to have a baby before I got married and to finish high school. I understood that if anything was to happen, it was up to me.

With time I came to understand that my mother really did love me and she tried her best with what she knew. I forgave her for abandoning me so many times as a child because it was a hardship she had also suffered. I cherished one gift Mom gave me: music. When I listened to music and especially when I sang, it took me to places far away from my problems, even if just for a moment. Until I started to sing professionally, I felt invisible. Singing lifted me up and brought me joy and I found out quickly that people actually liked to hear me sing. It felt good and when I was on stage, I finally felt accepted. One of my first gigs was at the MacDonald Hotel lounge in Edmonton. On a busy Saturday night, I remember just closing my eyes and singing this beautiful ballad. Usually when you sing in a lounge, you're background entertainment. People are always talking but you get used to that. On this particular night, when I finished, it was so quiet. I opened my eyes to find each person in the room looking at me. They'd really been listening to me sing and applauded so loudly it took me by surprise. Finally, I felt right at home.

After working together for about a year, I married my guitar player and we sang in a duo called Just Friends, travelling and playing clubs across western Canada. After being on the road for five years we started to get gigs at home. The following year I give birth to our son and then 13 months later our daughter was born. We struggled with our marriage after that and, in 1982 I found myself a divorced mother of two children under the age of three. I had come to understand that things change and sometimes do not turn out the way we hope.

During the next six years as a single mom I sang six nights a week and listened every afternoon to a talk show on CJCA called 'That's Living.' It was my only source of information about raising children and I appreciated all the advice I heard from Dr. Paterson, Dr. Blashko and Dr. Janzen, who slowly became my favorite host.

In 1986 I auditioned and was chosen as the first ever local ambassador for the City of Edmonton in the role of Klondike Kate. For two years I travelled the USA and Canada and sang at telethons, performed on radio and television, sang with Bobby Curtola in Las Vegas, starred in commercials, and performed at the Curling Championship Brier, and had the honour of singing the national anthems at both CFL and the Stanley Cup playoff games. I felt blessed to be able to take care of my children and make a good living in the music industry.

I realized that the gigs were starting to dry up at the end of my two-year term as Klondike Kate. I took time to be still and to visualize how things were going to get better for the kids and me - I did feel optimistic. Again, I knew that if something was going to happen it was up to me.

One day while driving downtown for a meeting with my booking agent, I had my radio tuned as always to That's Living. Dr. Janzen was on the air that day and sharing that his wife, who had struggled with cancer for the previous six months, had passed away. I remember it so clearly as he explained how he needed to come to work that day and to be on air so that he could help others, and how he hoped his listeners would understand. I cried like a baby.

Through my tears, I said a prayer out loud: "Father, why can't I meet a man like Dr. Janzen who needs me as much as I need him?"

One month later I'd forgotten all about my prayer, when CJCA called and asked me to emcee their annual Christmas Bureau Telethon at the Four Seasons Hotel. All the radio personalities, hosts, sportscasters, news anchors, and other staff were on stage with me as I led them in singing Christmas carols. We ended up raising $10,000 that day.

After the fundraiser, we were invited to go next door to the legion to celebrate. I was putting on my coat and a man came over and offered to help me. We started walking down the hotel hallway toward the door to the street, and once I heard him speak I recognized his voice. It was Hank Janzen, and yes, I was nervous!

I'd always pictured him as a wise old man with long white hair and beard. He didn't look like that at all. He was much younger than I thought, he was tall and good looking. I remember him being so sad and he told me how he didn't really feel like being there that day, but he was preparing to take his kids and their grandparents to Palm Springs the next day. It would be the first Christmas the kids would spend without their mother.

When we walked into the legion, two elderly couples at a table just inside the door called us over. The two men reached out and shook Hank's hand and said they were so sorry about him losing his wife. One woman spoke to me and said what a great Klondike Kate I was and that she loved it when my children were on stage with me because they were so cute. Then the other woman took my hand and looked at Hank and me and said, "You two make such a cute couple – you take good care of each other."

At that moment I actually looked up into Hank's eyes -really looked- and noticed they were a deep brown. He looked back at me, and it seemed like time stood still. All of a sudden, I remembered my prayer. He just smiled down at me. I was in awe.

Later Hank asked me if he could call me sometime. I gave him my phone number. Something amazing happened. He called the next night, and the next night and every night while he was away. Our conversations got longer each time he called, and we talked about *everything*. Our past, our faith in God, our values, our children, and our plans and hopes for the future. When he came home, I felt like we'd been dating for six months just because of all the long and meaningful conversations we'd had. We were married the following year and have been happily married ever since. I learned then that when you pray, be *very specific*!

I wanted to share my story with you, so that you understand that in order for me to cope with my circumstances as a child, and now as a business woman, I have to be still and to listen each time I am in transition. I have learned well how to wait and to embrace the change that inevitable comes. This has made me resilient and optimistic and in turn, so very grateful. Just like the little girl in the chapel at the convent, my adult self has a strong faith that things will work out as they need to and are meant to because that is what I envisioned. Even more importantly, whenever I am still, I listen to my gut and I feel gratitude for what I want as if it has already happened.

I listened when I decided to move away from home at fifteen. When I made the decision that it would be better and safer for my children if I divorced their father. When music gigs dwindled and I started to look for other opportunities. When I accepted Hank's marriage proposal. When I applied for university at thirty-seven years old. When after six years the permanent teaching positions didn't materialize and I decided to get my real estate license. When I took a course just this last year that will help me help others in their business. I recognized long ago that a life transition doesn't have to be seen as a failure; rather an opportunity to change and to grow.

As much as I hated waiting as a child, it prepared me well for my adult life. The waiting and being still is so much easier now; not as painful. As an adult I feel loved by the huge family I prayed for and finally got, I feel accepted by friends and coworkers, and I feel like I belong in the places that I create. So when I'm anxious, and yes it still happens, I take a few moments to be still; to breathe; to be grateful; to visualize what I want as if I already have it. I can tell you that when I truly believe and see my goal, whatever I'm worried about disappears. This special time gives me clarity and a better perspective about the problems or issues that I am facing. Sometimes I take only five minutes each day. I listen to what my body is telling me, notice the things I need to ignore or release, and if I'm feeling ignored or abandoned, I think about all the people in my life who love and support me and then dwell on all the things I'm grateful for. As a little girl, I did not have this kind of control over my life, but as a woman, I do.

Today I have a desire to be of service. To help others move through difficult situations and to help them take the time to be still so that they can understand, love and respect themselves and then focus on creating what they want - whether it is in their personal life or their career. I have met so many talented people who don't see their value or who see their transitions as failures. I want to encourage them, and you, that they're doing an amazing job. As a little girl, no one ever told me I was doing a good job or that things would get better. I want to be that voice for others and to show them that they're not alone.

I don't get stressed out anymore when circumstances prevent me from moving as fast as I would like. I know that sometimes the timing may not be right and I remember to be still; to listen and to wait.

I'm a survivor, and I know that you are too. You may be an entrepreneur embarking on a new business or a new adventure in your current business, or perhaps you are considering a change. You want to be your best, to be of service to others, and you want to belong to something bigger than yourself. As you strive for all of this, I encourage you also to take the time to be still. Louise Hay says to visualize what you want as if you already have it and to have a feeling of gratitude.

Just to put this in perspective, some of the things I visualized and prayed for didn't happen: I didn't find my father, I didn't become a huge recording artist, I didn't get a long term teaching contract, and I didn't become a top realtor (not yet!). But I am good enough, and so are you, no matter what. I am continually grateful for the prayers that have been answered and for the miracles that I see each and every day in my life; in my children and grandchildren's lives.

My daughter had her first baby in 2012 but when her baby girl was only 8 weeks old, she stopped breathing. The miracle is that although my daughter found a blue and non-responsive baby in the crib, the baby was revived and survived near SIDS -sudden infant death syndrome. The next 5 weeks were spent in ICU at the Stollery Childrens' Hospital. I spent the first three days just terrified for my daughter and for the baby; we were told the baby may not make it. On day four we were told that the baby would survive but that because of the severe brain damage from the lack of oxygen, she would not see, or walk and that she would probably need a feeding tube. Today, our precious angel is four years old and has Cerebral Palsy but she can walk with a walker and just started play school. She has cortical visual impairment;

her eyes are fine but her brain only allows her to see light and some colours. She is such a happy little girl; a miracle who brings us joy each and every day.

There is so much I am grateful for. I have the security that I never had as a child, I have a loving, faithful husband, I have the most incredible children and grandchildren who bless me every single day, I have a career that I love and I get to work with people I love.

We all go through difficult times and face hurdles that we must overcome in our business and personal life. Remember to take the time to be still, to listen, and to wait. Love yourself. Be still and enjoy the time alone with *you*. Be grateful. Visualize and really believe that you already have what you want and need. Be still. When the time is right you will become the bold and beautiful person you were meant to be and a beautiful and shining light to everyone around you.

Zandra Bell

Awarding winning motivational humorist, Zandra Bell stands for bringing 'joy to the job,' creating inspirational hilarity customized to her clients' workplace challenges and corporate reality.

Designed to unite and empower her audiences, Zandra's keynote presentations are the best solution to resolving stress, maximizing employee engagement and boosting staff productivity. Client testimonials proclaim, "Zandra Bell is face hurting funny."

In demand, as well, as an innovative marketing mentor, Zandra combines her creative vision with her brilliant wordsmithing to enlighten entrepreneurs on the art of 'Ingenious Business Revitalization.' International best-selling author, speaking talent and business success catalyst, Zandra is simply 'creativity' personified!

On the web www.zandrabell.com

On Facebook Facebook.com/InspirationalHilarity

ca.LinkedIn.com/in/zandrabell

Chapter 19

You Eat What You Kill

By Zandra Bell

So, you want the truth? The proverbial pig without the lipstick? The answer to what it really takes to build a business put forth as blatantly as it states in this book title, sans its usual layer of B...ah, bovine excrement.

(Hmmm. Why do all these familiar expressions involve barnyard animals?)

Well, if you ask me, the truth is that building a successful business is all in your mind!

So what does this mean? That it's just a fantasy, an impossibility, an act of insanity? Now, that's getting close...to the daily reality of it all, anyway. Before I address these astute inquiries, however, some background information wouldn't go amiss.

As a creative wordsmith and an expert at what I call 'fearless marketing' I serve my clients in many ways, one of which is designing effective and innovative promotional materials. While I was collaborating recently with a professional bookkeeper on her video e-course, reviewing what she had compiled and handed in to me so I could work my magic, I had to put a halt to her enthusiastic explanations because I realized that her proposed copy was totally over the heads of her potential audience. It assumed that all the eager entrepreneurs who would ultimately be viewing this instructional material would already have that strange and elusive thing called...now, say it after me... a... business... plan.

No one has a business *plan*. Well, the bookkeeper does, evidently. But, you know, normal people. They may have something akin to it that they paid some consultant to devise which has long since ceased to have any relevancy to what is actually happening in their business, even though it was only completed last week.

Ok, I admit to being somewhat facetious here, but, seriously, in response to her incredulity that individuals would actually start up a business without knowing the facts, without having a plan on paper to see whether it would succeed or fail, I conducted a survey.

No one has a business plan.

Perhaps, after some time in operation, they might now be developing one, because they think it just might be the key to actually making a profit. Personally, however, I think that if I had to face the truth, to look down and see in black and white, the black hole I was walking into when I left the security and paid benefits of my government management position to throw myself into the hopefully merciful arms of the Universe and pursue a life of empowering corporate audiences with humour completely customized to their workplace realities, challenges and frustrations, well, I would have just spent my meager remaining credit card balance on more psychotherapy. Working for the government, it can suck out your brain.

I tried to formulate a plan. I did, but the way I see it, you can fuss and stress and plot and prepare and still do nothing…out of fear. That old 'paralysis by analysis' chestnut. Did you know that worry is negative prayer?

My mother was a chronic planner. There we were, enjoying the Dixieland jazz at the Air Force club, or so I thought, until I noticed her furrowed brow and obvious agitation. When I inquired as to her discomfiture, she responded that, now get this, she was busy plotting out the route through the chairs she was going to take the next time she had to go to the bathroom. Did she have to go now? No, she just wanted to be prepared. Way to live in the moment, Mom!

Ah, how we waste our precious energy on worrying about some nebulous eventuality that may not even come to pass. Can you think of anything more unproductive? By the time she's actually needing to use the bathroom, people will have come and gone, and the chairs will be in a totally different configuration ruthlessly thwarting her carefully conceived strategy. All that wasted time and angst, when she could have just been happy.

And, bottom line, when you really have to go to the bathroom, when have mere tables and chairs ever stood in your way?

It's a metaphor for life. Sort of like that old saying, you know, I'd rather die peacefully like my grandfather in his sleep, not screaming in terror like the passengers in his car. See, same outcome, but who had the better time? Deal with the details as they happen. You don't need to depress yourself by anticipating disaster. In fact, negative thinking is only going to bring disaster about.

Roy Osing asserts in his book, '*Be Different or Be Dead*: *Execute First Plan Second.*'

"Unfortunately, the Plan, regardless of how pristine or intellectually clever it is, does not guarantee a win. ...Results are achieved 'out there' in the trenches where stuff is delivered to people... Winning is messy, inelegant and, yes, painful.

Winning is achieved by people doing things, not thinking things... a function of Brilliant EXECUTION, not what's on paper."

You want progress, not perfection, if you ever want to get anywhere, or do anything in business.

So, finally, fully aware that I had no savings, no income and even less of an idea as to what I was doing, I just ripped off the Band-Aid and jumped, my hands over my eyes. A friend, at the time, had even insisted that I couldn't survive without bi-weekly paychecks, not being the 'starving artist' type. True. But, why does an artist need to starve?

I subsequently innovated a whole new approach to motivational speaking, entwining comedy into the business realm, creating inspirational hilarity designed to reduce stress, raise morale, inspire employee engagement and thus increase staff productivity for a better company bottom line.

My hilarious alter ego, 'Shirley Best,' quickly began garnering rave reviews at popular arts festivals and traveling to key note engagements all over North America, comedy royalty on the conference scene. Twice voted Funniest Edmontonian, honoured as a Global Television Woman of Vision, at one point, I was on the cover of three prominent local publications at the same time!

It was fabulous! I was embracing it all. Grateful for it all, I definitely wanted it to continue, except for a tiny, niggling misgiving. What if everyone realized I was an imposter? Not an incredibly talented star at all, just the bad, selfish, undeserving, neglected little girl, who tried so desperately to get her parents to notice her, to love her, to no avail. Everyone enthused that I was so intelligent, so funny, so deserving of my own TV show. I was seeking bigger, better speaking opportunities. Why was my career only going so far, when I wanted so much more?

In retrospect, I would say that my inside reality just hadn't caught up to my outside one. Truthfully, at that point, I *thought* I was running a business but, what with times being 'tops' and everything going my way, I didn't need to think of those practical things like marketing and money management. I didn't even *think* to think of them! Just a clueless little upstart startup, I was working *in* my business, hell yeah! But never *on* it. I didn't know what I didn't know.

Bringing home the bacon, living high off the hog, it's damn easy to be profitable when the times they are a thrivin'.

(You see what I mean about this barnyard animal idiom allure, although, under closer scrutiny, perhaps it's predominately more porcine for some inexplicable reason.)

When the economy downturns, and familial responsibilities dictate that you need to focus attention elsewhere, devote your time to raising your elderly parents, 'geriatric whispering' as I like to refer to it, that's when you soon realize that no matter how amazingly talented and sought after you are, the reality is outta sight, outta mind, baby!

Welcome to the entrepreneurial jungle, where the stark reality is this: You Eat What You Kill. You are no longer an inside cat, with a constant stream of cream, and a cushy pillow to curl up upon while you luxuriate in licking your 'lady partsicles' under the auspices of 'grooming.'

No! Now, you're an outside cat, prowling for a paycheck, out there in those aforementioned trenches marketing your prey, praying for a sale, considering yourself lucky if you can even afford to get your roots coloured before the grey starts showing again because you don't have any extra money and you certainly don't have the time.

Of course, when you finally do make the sale, you celebrate wildly (yeah, right) by working twenty hour days to get the project finished for the client whose flagrant procrastination has forced them to hire you and now they need the work done now, now, NOW! They always want instant gratification. Oh no, sorry, that would take too long.

Adding insult to injury, is the buttock clenching frustration of having clients who, despite the previously agreed upon terms of the contract, now for some reason can't or won't pay! A solopreneur has no recourse. What are you going to do? Take them to court? It would cost more than they owe. It's the *principle of the thing*!

Hey it gets worse. Now, let's assume they do pay, by cheque, so archaic, but big corporations still use them, however, banks now often refuse them. If they cannot telephone, on the spot, the signatory, his workplace supervisor and every member of his professional association, extended family and fantasy football team, not to mention the entire staff of the bank where the cheque originated, for security purposes, of course, well then, despite the fact that you've had an account there for twenty years and have never gone into overdraft, they are going to have to hold funds for 10 days.

I once had them insist upon doing this with a cheque that was written on their own bank! Issued through their very city corporation itself!

It can be brutal out there, not the reward you were expecting for all your exigent efforts, the hard driving dedication that propels you to be out there, every day, working like a dog. It just makes you want to lift your leg.

No one alerts you either that, at a certain point in life, your parents become your children. I had no idea. I never wanted children. As my comedic alter ego, Shirley Best, would claim, "Come on, suffer extreme pain to birth forth your own rival!? Sounds like a Greek tragedy to me." The simple truth was that, after my mother's passing, my father needed me more and more as he aged and I just couldn't leave him all alone.

No matter how dedicated I remained to my business, something was bound to slip when I was continually commuting between two provinces on a bi-weekly basis to act as his caregiver, a situation that not only compromised my freedom, decimated my finances, but also plunged me back into the inanities of my dysfunctional family. The crab claw of responsibility had pulled me back down into the bucket.

It certainly was a time for 'aha moments' however. On the outside, the quality of my creative work never faltered. Inside, however, I was undergoing one of the most transformational experiences of my lifetime, new and deeper understandings blossoming in their divine timing. My personal ordeal served as a catalyst, forcing me to question long held beliefs, and dig deep within for answers. Despite all outside odds, I was starting to believe in the uniquely amazing, wildly talented person that was ME.

My 'inside reality' was catching up.

To meet the new external challenges, I turned my creative gifts to marketing and promotion in order to more effectively convey my message, the incredible value of using humour in business, to an altered world of ideal clients, they, themselves, fighting to survive in a depressed economy. You can't change what's happening in your office, in your organization, but there's no better tool than targeted humour to change the way your people *react* to it!

Making a positive difference, that's what I do.

To survive the vagaries of today's world, entrepreneurs need to continually reinvent themselves, their businesses and their whole approach to client attraction on a regular basis. My strategy to maintain the level of success I'd achieved was to devise an entirely new and different branch of my main business. Utilizing my wordsmithing talents, unique perspective and imaginative, 'out of the box' thinking, I focused on helping other entrepreneurs communicate their own solutions in a more concise, compelling manner so that, ultimately, they could up-level their operations and increase sales.

'Ingenious Business Revitalization' as I call it, is an inventive, objective look at your business which results in you, its owner, learning how to get out there and play a bigger, better game.

In the past, I'd always been the one to provide help to others, especially financial support. One of the most difficult lessons I had to learn was how to *receive* help, especially financial support. We're socialized to believe it's a sign of weakness and failure. Au contraire, I emphatically assure you! In fact, I came to realize that it was actually all part of the divine ebb and flow, the give and take of the Universe. It just makes sense.

Here we are out there in that entrepreneurial jungle, by choice, essentially asking for the opportunities, collaborations, clients, and sales that we need to survive. I won't even mention the whinging, wailing and gnashing of teeth that regularly takes place while we strive, struggle and then wait impatiently for it all to come, thereby pushing it all away, by the way, à la Law of Attraction, 'like' attracting 'like' and all.

What is all of the above but energy being focused on the great, big LACK? In the midst of all this, here comes someone in your time of need who offers to help, financially or otherwise, and what is the typical response? 'Oh no, that's ok. Really, I'm fine. I don't need your help.'

Yes, you do! What is in the way? Pride, outmoded beliefs, sheer stupidity!? We're constantly asking for everything from those outside forces, you know, Fate, Luck, the Universe, God. Well, did it ever occur to you that this person's generosity might just be the way all these so-called forces were planning on responding!?

And you said NO. A big NO to the flow of abundance trying to come your way. Are you insane?

Again, in the whole Law of Attraction scheme of things, saying no to *some* help and abundance means saying no to *all* help and abundance and that will never do. An 'outside cat' must keep the channels to divine intervention open and flowing. Refusing help, energetically speaking, is biting the hand that feeds you, looking that great big gift horse in the mouth.

(Ok, not just pigs, definitely animal farm.)

One business Rubik's Cube that I've yet to solve is the old 'time management/achieving life work balance' quandary. All the popular pundits vow it's achievable, but, if you ask me, the concept of doing it all and having it all is one big steamy cowpie.

Sure, I, too, want it all. Hell, I want it delivered!

But, when you're working intently on that greater goal, it only follows that something has got to give, something is going to slip through the cracks, certain aspects of your business or personal life are going to be compromised. Don't get so preoccupied over everyone else looking like they have it all together. Trust me, they don't.

Don't judge your inside reality by someone else's outside one. You have no idea what their life is really like. Maybe they're so swamped keeping up that front, they can't even remember their children's names. Whereas you see your own doubts, fears, inadequacies and insecurities as if they're magnified a hundred times, so don't torture yourself! It's not a fair comparison. We're all on our own path. It's a matter of establishing priorities and making choices. Decide what you want and go after it.

Because the truth is that building a successful business really *is* all in your mind!

You cannot achieve success on the outside unless you believe you deserve success on the inside. The good news is that you have the power right there in your 'desperately in need of a manicure' hands, the power to create the business of your dreams, the *life* of your dreams, but it takes courage, focus, perseverance, and tremendous mental self-discipline.

On the outside there's the inhumane deadlines, working weekends, the endless networking, forcing yourself to be ON, positive, perky, smiley when you rather be home curled up on your comfy couch...grooming.

Standing for hours, your feet like little raw and swollen pot roasts crammed into those stylish but impractical high heels. Juggling plate, napkin and wine glass in an effort to shake hands with potential business contacts without spilling Merlot down your stain magnet silk blouse. Desperately hoping you can get through the trite party repartee without inadvertently spitting out bits of hors d'oeuvres onto someone's lapel. It's really obvious when it hits their name tag. There's just no coming back from that.

On the inside, you have to, above all, have *faith*. Never allow yourself to become discouraged or depressed because, again, 'like' attracts 'like,' and you don't want to slide into that downward spiral. Always remain confident, optimistic, ambitious and enthusiastic. Keep your imagination centered on your goal and your faith moving towards it.

Remember, everything *is* possible. The only obstacle preventing you from building that successful business is you.

I won't lie and say it's easy, even when you know what to do.

Do you always get what you want? Absolutely not, but you always get what you need. You just might not realize that at the time.

Would I give it all up and go get a job? Relinquish the opportunity to fulfill my potential, explore my creativity, strut my talents? Would I dim my light and cease to shine?

When pigs fly, baby, when pigs fly.

Conclusion

Kate: so, there you have it! The no bullshit and truth from bold game changers in the business. The wisdom within these pages is exactly what you need to help inspire and impact your world with TRUTH! Not the "How to build a 6-figure business in 6 days" rubbish that flies out at you each time you open your newsfeed.

These are the blood, sweat and tears of women who have worked their butts off and understand the true nature of what it takes to succeed. I am so happy to have taken this journey with Kim and these ladies to fetch you the real raw truth.

Do take all these years of wisdom and advice and apply them to your life and business the best way you can. There is no better teacher then experience, and this book is jam packed full of it.

Kim: Here you are all 18 of us, sharing all the B.S. we went through and go through to keep growing and evolving! However, I hope when you read this book, you also begin to minimize and stop the unnecessary B.S. in your life! We are all here together to support - there is enough business in this world for everyone. Show up strong and proud! Make sure you can look into the mirror and say "I love You. I am honest and I Do the WORK- Personally and Professionally." (By the way, those two areas are not separate, they are one!) Stay true to you, and you will not go wrong. Remove judgment of others and allow them to be where they are in life. Live by the Four Agreements! We all have lessons to learn, ups and downs to go through. Do not sell yourself out for one more minute of any Book of Law bullshit! Stop playing small, be responsible and surround yourself with the other like-minded peeps!

This is myself and Kate's last anthology - retirement here we come. We have compiled many of these books. We have grown, learned a lot and faced plenty of BS in these projects. It is time for us to go on to bigger platforms to support others. I must say, it has been a bumpy ride, but for me personally, I wouldn't change a thing!

Welcome to a digital magazine

like NO OTHER!

The Missing Piece Magazine is an interactive digital self-discovery magazine where you will be opened to powerful information and exercises to accompany you on your self-discovery journey. The Missing Piece Magazine also helps online business owners, coaches, and mentors to be positioned in front of 'highly' targeted audience by presenting themselves and their knowledge our network coverage of over 300,000 people per month.

START YOUR JOURNEY TO SOMETHING WONDERFUL!

www.TheMissingPieceMagazine.com

The Bold Authority Builder

Become the Expert in YOUR Business!

Have your business running like a well-oiled machine! Reduce your stress, increase your time, set up strong business boundaries, elevate your confidence and receive what you are worth! Step into your CEO with strength and confidence.

If you need help with:

- Organizational Structures

- Customize Processes

- Business Vision & Mission

- Time Management

- Up-Leveling Your CEO

- Stress Reduction

- Strengthening Your Brand & Expertise

- Increase Your Visibility

- Streamline Your Marketing

If you are already an existing business owners who needs detailed help to create smart organizational plans to increase your reach and grow your revenue; you're in business and you want to grow your business to the next level with strategic implementations, great! Now is the time to do this!

Visit www.kimbsmith.com today!

N

The End